A Time to Seek

A Time to Seek

Fascinating
New Insights
in the Torah

RABBI BARUCH DOV BRAUN

Mosaica Press, Inc.
© 2018 by Mosaica Press
Designed and typeset by Brocha Mirel Strizower

ISBN-10: 1-946351-27-X
ISBN-13: 978-1-946351-27-2

All rights reserved. No part of this book may be used or reproduced or transmitted in any form or by any means, electronic or mechanical, including photocopying, recording, or by any information storage and retrieval system, without written permission from the publisher.

Published and distributed by:
Mosaica Press, Inc.
www.mosaicapress.com
info@mosaicapress.com

Dedicated by

YOSSI AND TZIPPY PELEG BILLIG

Our prophets emphasized over and over again the mitzvos between man and his fellow.

The prophet Michah says:

הִגִּיד לְךָ אָדָם מַה טּוֹב וּמָה יְקֹוָק דּוֹרֵשׁ מִמְּךָ כִּי אִם עֲשׂוֹת מִשְׁפָּט וְאַהֲבַת חֶסֶד וְהַצְנֵעַ לֶכֶת עִם אֱלֹקֶיךָ

In the beginning of his prophecy, Yeshayahu says:

גַּם כִּי תַרְבּוּ תְפִלָּה אֵינֶנִּי שֹׁמֵעַ יְדֵיכֶם דָּמִים מָלֵאוּ רַחֲצוּ הִזַּכּוּ הָסִירוּ רֹעַ מַעַלְלֵיכֶם מִנֶּגֶד עֵינָי חִדְלוּ הָרֵעַ

May we all heed the message of the prophets.

Then, we will merit *achdus* and *shalom bayis* in our midst.

DRS. ROSALIE AND LEON REICH
are proud of our revered rabbi

Rabbi Baruch Dov Braun

and
his book that includes a compilation of his inspiring *derashot*.
We are certain that the book will continue to inspire its readers for
many years to come.

In honor of

Elliot Braun
אליהו בן ברוך ורבקה

In memory of

Eva Lux Braun
עלא גיטל בת יצחק שמעון ודבורה

Sandor Freud
שלמה בן אליעזר וחיה

Amalia Freud
מליא בת יוסף יהודה ורחל

JUDY AND YITZ BRAUN
Proud parents of Rabbi Baruch Dov Braun

This *sefer* is dedicated to the memory of
שמואל בן ר' דוד
Samuel Ehrenhalt
Beloved Husband, Father, and Grandfather
Supporter of Israel
Lifelong Student

ELEANOR EHRENHALT
DINA AND DAVID STEINBERG
HEATHER AND STEVEN EHRENHALT

Dedicated by
LOUIS AND CEIL GROSSMAN

In honor of our parents
Abraham and Thelma Wadler

In memory of
Munysz and Frida Grossman

We are extremely proud of our dear son-in-law
Rabbi Baruch Dov Braun
on his accomplishment of publishing his first *sefer*.
May he continue to have success in all his future endeavors.

Seth and Esther Grossman

and Family

לז"נ

דוד בן מנחם מוניש

לז״נ

In memory of

מאיר בן שלום דוב

Michael Simanowitz

Mikey was our dear, compassionate, generous, kind, funny, and loyal friend who led every day of his life by example. Our spirits were always lifted when he was around, and we cherish the relationship we were able to have with him and his family.

His widespread loving-kindness and sensitivity to everyone he encountered will have a long-reaching impact, never to be forgotten.

הנחה את עמו בארח מישור

May his blessed memory be a source of comfort for his family.
Forever in our hearts,

ABE AND SIMONE PORT

MEIR AND ERIN

RENA PORT

לז״נ

שמעון בן צבי מנחם

שרה בת שמשון הכהן

and

חיים זאב בן טובי

בילע בת יום טוב ליפי

DEDICATED BY THE PUDERBEUTEL FAMILY

In loving memory of

Mr. and Mrs. Nathan Silver

and

Mr. and Mrs. Samuel Monderer

In loving memory of

Dr. Joseph Silver

and

Dr. Isaac Belizon

לז"נ

נפתלי חיים בן משה צבי ע"ה

Naftali Trauring

He was a man totally dedicated to his family and his love for Israel. He was kind, honest, and gentle, but a force and leader of the family. We miss him very much.

ANNIE TRAURING
HELEN AND JACOB WEICHHOLZ
JORDANA AND BENJAMIN STAIMAN AND FAMILY
DEVORI AND DANI WEICHHOLZ AND FAMILY
LILY AND MICHAEL WEICHHOLZ AND FAMILY

EVELYN AND STANLEY WEISS

In memory of our parents

Jean and Marvin Ehrenberg *a"h*

Ruth and Louis Weiss *a"h*

who held Torah scholarship in high regard in their lives.

RABBI NAFTALI JAEGER
Rosh HaYeshiva

בס"ד ב' אלול תשס"א

אגרת ברכה

דעת ועצה כי אם פעם אחת קיום עולה זה אמרו לבית הלוי ולדבר יקרא
על כן האומרים כגון דאשתום ועלמה לבית הלוי ואם בינה [?] היא
עולה גב בסוד העולה והכסף והנחשת ואלו הדברים כלולים בהלכות העולה

לענין יעבץ הבא"ה לדבר הנה ברוך דלך רבי הגאון [?] הגדול וגם לגאון
בעלים. עומד הוא הפקוד לאמר"י לכך נאמרו ודע גילוי המר(ס) כד נזכר
אצל הגאון אביר הפלאה רבי יצחק והלכה לכם החכמה והלכת ושלמתי
אתכל אברהם של עמך ישרון והסר לא ברצו להגיד הנועד ונטעת בתוך הלבבות
לשם באמתך יד ולהגאון הב כ' נאמר בזה ק' הוא ק' יה' רצח של
כמוסה - טל - ומלא [? ?] אגל אגד בני עולם בית אמרו גם' רב ודגול רגלי אהרן
וכלי מטה וכלי עבודים היה הכלסי' רב ועלמה דרך בית דלתי ודגל
אל ברכת לגוף העולה ולקראת שלום שלשה

לענין כנור' אבל אמרו דאתני [?] דיין בסגנה. אף הנקרא
אבודו רחם אל עבודה וגדולי שלבה ואין הוא אקמונות[?] וסגנו הגרב
לשונו אומר כי לקראת שלום הנועד שלרות אחד אהל עולה של א ישראל
ועולים אני עם נסאב הא ישראל הז אהל מקבל ומעכי מיצירי
וסבל כלו אמת שלים ובכן האמרגי ולא חצין אמגן . ויהיה בכה לבי אחרים
מאדה להאקר ולדגוה. ועלקדבית מלאכת אדיה אומר נעשה כבי ונגל
להבה הכבוד לעולם ולמכה לענין יותר כם כך. בכלין ולהאייר עולמים הרבה
כשם ישר [?] לענין בעלוה אנשים ובורך [?] ובכת באלאגדי שעריך אין אגרא
אמלך בדואיט מינוחת הנפש ולשמחה

לברכת הדברים הדולי לעצמי אצל דלותי ד"ר ואגדל
ודולה הדולי. לדברים הולידים ולצל לית דר' ה' ליולג. לדבר ולהליעצו לרבי שלדולג הבורא.

נפתלי יעגר
דרבנן דולם לכום

ONE CEDARLAWN AVENUE • LAWRENCE, NY 11559 • (516) 239-9002 • FAX: (516) 239-9003

YESHIVA UNIVERSITY

Wilf Campus, Glueck Center, Room 312 | New York, NY 10033 | Phone 212.5007007

Rabbi Dr. Michael Rosensweig
Department of Talmud

Mazer Yeshiva Program/RIETS

בס"ד
יום ב' לפרשת וירא, תשע"ח

I was exceedingly pleased to receive several chapters of Rabbi Baruch Dov Braun's forthcoming *sefer*, which contains *derashot* on *parshat ha-shavua*. The discourses are written in a clear style and thoughtful manner. They constitute insightful essays on classical and timeless issues in halakhic life that also particularly resonate in contemporary circumstances. These presentations are deeply rooted in the classical sources of the Gemara, midrash, and *parshanut* of the Rishonim, but are also effectively supplemented by later *mekorot*, as well. The works of the Seforno, Maharal, Or haHayim haKadosh, the Netziv, Rav Hirsch, Kedushat Levi, and Rav Soloveitchik, among others, are invoked to reinforce important *hashkafic* conclusions that are particularly relevant in our era.

Rabbi Baruch Dov Braun is a fine young *talmid hakham*, who is making important contributions in the world of *hinukh* and *rabbanut*. He learned diligently in our yeshivah, Yeshivat Rabbenu Yitzhak Elhanan, and he excelled as a *talmid* in my *shiur* and in the Kollel Elyon for numerous years. I am pleased to recommend his forthcoming *sefer* which projects timeless Torah values that are especially vital in our time. May he and his family continue to grow in *avodat Hashem* and *harbazat haTorah*, להגדיל תורה ולהאדירה.

בברכת התורה

מיכאל רוזנצווייג
ראש ישיבה וראש כולל
ישיבת רבינו יצחק אלחנן

For

Mom & Dad

Table of Contents

Foreword XXI
Acknowledgments XXIII
Introduction 1

Bereishis
A Threat to Parenthood 5
Hevel's Approach to Life's Brevity 10

Noach
The Perils of Caretaking 13
Noach and the Wonderful Wizard of Oz 17
A Second Chance 25

Lech Lecha
Redefining Chessed 30

Vayeira
Glancing Back: Curiosity or Concern? 35

Chayei Sarah
Minchah's Contribution 39

Toldos
The US Constitution, Megillas Esther, and Eisav 43

Vayeitzei
Who's Carrying Who? 49
Influential Images 54

XVIII   A Time to Seek

Vayishlach
The Anonymous Hero 57

Vayeishev
Glue Is More Righteous than Velcro 61

Mikeitz
A Silent Prayer. 66

Vayigash
A (Not So) Different Kind of Shema 70

Vayechi
From Rags to Riches. 74
Blessings and Brexit. 79

Shemos
The Parashah with No Names. 85
Dancing Children 90

Va'eira
A Visit to the Egyptian Zoo. 96

Bo
The Politics of Citizenship. 102

Beshalach
Singing Angels, Robots, and Humans 110

Yisro
The Difference Between Yisro and Balak. 115
A Timeless Protest 119

Mishpatim
When Law Is Not Free from Passion 122

Terumah
Authenticity vs. Sincerity 126

Tetzaveh
The Sights and Sounds of Mitzvos 131

Ki Sisa
Counting and Complacency 136
Pilgrimage, Jews, and Judaism 141
Zemiros, Shiros, V'Torah. 144

Vayakhel-Pekudei
Mirror, Mirror, on the Kiyur. 147
Grammar and Greatness 153

Foreword

A PROMINENT RABBI of the previous generation, famed for his ability to teach adults, was asked for the secret of his success. Nothing magical, he said, only two things: First, make time for your own learning, *lishmah*; second, read widely. Do this, and you will always have something to say and find a way to say it.

Rabbi Braun's collection of *derashot* testifies that these methods are effective not only in teaching but in preaching as well. His book is not a work of pure *lomdut*, nor is it a series of essays in *parshanut ha-mikra*, nor is it a treatise on social, political, and cultural issues. At the same time, it could not have been produced were it not for the author's assiduousness in *talmud Torah* — despite the many duties of the rabbinate and teaching — which is not limited to the *massekhtot* he teaches but embraces a broad range of topics from *Moed* through *Kodashim*, on which he continues to keep "active files." Likewise, his preaching reflects an awareness of *peshuto shel mikra*, and his references to contemporary life benefit from genuine curiosity, serious reading, and social-work experience.

Rabbi Braun's goal is to show how the complexity and depth of Torah can be applied to the task of daily living. He writes about the need to discover a richer and more precise "vocabulary," informed by Torah. Vocabulary does not simply mean a list of dictionary definitions of exotic words. It means acquiring concepts and images and associations that provide a "sound track" for our lives and tools for our edification.

To take three examples almost at random: *Ramban* held that the name Hevel derives from the Hebrew word for mist but that his mother, in naming him, did not explain the name because it implies the transience, hence futility, of life. We contemplate the transience of life when we read *Kohelet* — all life is mist (*hevel*). How indeed do we find value in a transient existence? Rabbi Braun works out the logic of *Ramban*'s laconic remark: From one perspective, human beings wish to "dim the lights" and avoid confronting the brevity of existence. At the same time, a transient life can become a life lived with a sense of urgency, which is the opposite of despondency. As I have paraphrased it, this is a complex idea. Yet the image Rabbi Braun presents — the gap between our awareness of transience and our ability to live meaningfully with that awareness, represented by Hava giving a name while shying away from explaining it, conveys the idea memorably.

Noah remained "alone" (*akh*) in the ark, charged with the care of the animals entrusted to him. *Rashi* elaborated on three connotations of the Hebrew word. Rabbi Braun uses these three interpretations to capture succinctly three aspects of one of the great challenges most of us will face at some time or another in caring for persons we love who are no longer able to care for themselves. We are left with a vivid encapsulation of the difficulties we must deal with.

Rabbi Braun frequently reflects on the fact that our general society is marked by a retreat from traditional family life with its stress on the permanence of marriage. The high incidence of divorce and its effect on children is one salient feature of our culture. This becomes the subject of Rabbi Braun's sermon on the separation and remarriage of Amram and Yocheved. The image that Rabbi Braun focuses on and brings to life is that of the small child Aaron dancing at his parents' remarriage.

I am pleased that this book will bring Rabbi Braun's approach to the attention of a broader audience. I look forward to his continued productivity as a *talmid hakham* and *marbitz Torah*.

Shalom Carmy

Acknowledgments

FIRST AND FOREMOST, I would like to express my gratitude to the Ribbono Shel Olam for everything that He has granted me.

It is a privilege to serve as the rabbi of Young Israel of Avenue J. Thank you to the president, Avrumie Gross, and to all the members of the shul for the close relationships we've developed over the years and for affording me the opportunity to teach and learn Torah with you. Your positive feedback regarding my *derashos* and *shiurim* encouraged me to publish them for a wider audience.

Thank you, to all my *rebbeim* who have inspired me to make learning and teaching Torah my vocation.

Thank you, Rav Ari, Elie, and Doni Marcus, for having such a positive influence on me as a young man. At Yeshivat Reishit Yerushalayim, my love of learning began to flourish.

Thank you, Rav Naftali Jaeger, for the interest you showed in my spiritual development and for the vivid example of learning *b'hasmadah* that has left a lasting impression on me. The warmth of the *beis midrash* at Yeshiva Shor Yoshuv provided me with an environment to develop my learning skills and deepen my relationship with Hashem.

Thank you, Rav Michael Rosensweig, for the transformative effect you have had on me. It wasn't until I was introduced to your *shiurim*, with their unique methodology and focus, that I started to consider a career in the rabbinate. As a result, I came to Yeshiva University's Rabbi Isaac Elchanan Theological Seminary (RIETS) to pursue *semichah* and to learn in your *shiur*. Seven years later, I left as a *musmach* and a bona fide *talmid* of yours.

Thank you, Rav Baruch Simon, for your dedication to developing young rabbis in the RIETS *semichah* program. It is assuring to know that you are always available to offer guidance and to answer any questions I may have.

Thank you, Rabbi Dr. Richard Weiss, for mentoring me throughout my tenure at Young Israel of Hillcrest. The way you interact with your *mispallelim*, your scholarship, and the style of your *derashos* have served as a model for me in my position.

Thank you, Rav Shalom Carmy, for all the encouragement, motivation, and mentoring you have given me ever since I arrived at the shul. Ironically, my rabbinic position in Young Israel of Avenue J led me to finding another *rebbi*.

Thank you to all the generous sponsors who made this book possible: Mr. and Mrs. Yossi and Tzippy Peleg Billig, Mr. and Mrs. Yitz and Judy Braun, Mrs. Eleanor Erenhalt, Mr. and Mrs. Steven and Heather Erenhalt, Mr. and Mrs. Shmuel and Naomi Goldstein, Mr. and Mrs. Louis and Ceil Grossman, Rabbi and Mrs. Seth and Esther Grossman, Dr. and Mrs. Abraham and Simone Port, Mrs. Rena Port, Mr. and Mrs. Murray and Fran Puderbeutel, Mr. and Mrs. Shlomo and Barbara Rabinowitz, Drs. Leon and Rosalie Reich, Mr. and Mrs. Gerald and Helen Silver, Mr. and Mrs. David and Dina Steinberg, Dr. and Mrs. Herb and Sue Taragin, Mrs. Anita Walker, Dr. and Mrs. Dani and Devori Weichholz, Mr. and Mrs. Jacob and Helen Weichholz, Dr. and Mrs. Stanley and Evelyn Weiss.

It has been a pleasure working with Mosaica Press to bring this book to light. Rabbi Doron Kornbluth believed in this project from the start, meticulously reviewed the manuscript and offered helpful comments and suggestions. This book would not be the same if not for the staff at Mosaica Press.

I first began to discover my writing potential in Professor Leslie S. Newman's rabbinic writing course at RIETS. Long after leaving her classroom, Professor Newman not only encouraged me to further develop my writing skills, she also sacrificed much of her time to edit some of my previous essays in order to help me improve my skills.

I was enabled to study Torah intensively and develop a wide range of pastoral skills at RIETS for seven years thanks to the generosity of Ms. Susan Wexner. The Bella and Harry Wexner Kollel Elyon and Semikhah

Honors Program, with its array of courses from rabbinic counseling to public speaking, were indispensible to my development as a rabbi.

I am fortunate to be able to teach Torah on a daily basis at Davis Renov Stahler Yeshiva High School for Boys (DRS), under the auspices of Rabbi Yisroel Kaminetsky and Rabbi Elly Storch. In DRS, I am given the flexibility to share with my students an interdisciplinary style of learning. My students' interest in my lessons has encouraged me to publish for a broader audience.

I have been blessed to be part of a warm and loving family.

As Holocaust survivors, my grandparents, Saba and Savta, Mr. and Mrs. Eliyahu, *ybc"l*, and Eva Lux Braun, *a"h*, and Apu and Anyu, Mr. and Mrs. Sandor and Amalya Freud, *a"h*, instilled in me the importance of having *emunah* coupled with ambition. Growing up, their endless giving and involvement in my life from one milestone to the next was invaluable to my development.

The English poet Robert Browning wrote, "Ah, but a man's *reach* should exceed his grasp, or what's a *heaven* for?" My dear parents have enabled me to chase my dreams. None of my achievements would have been possible if not for their unconditional love and support. Thank you, Mom and Dad. This book is dedicated to you.

In addition to my parents, I am fortunate to have loving and supportive in-laws. They always encourage me to pursue my ambitions and express their pride in all my accomplishments. Thank you, Ima and Abba.

To my brother, brothers-in-law, and sisters-in-law, Eliezer and Shaina Braun, Yaakov and Sara Grossman, and Shmuel and Chana Grossman: Thank you for the memorable moments our families share together and for your interest in all my endeavors.

Hashem has blessed me with my *eishes chayil*, Nechama. Her modesty prevents me from further elaboration. Instead, I offer this: What's mine and yours, is hers.

To my dear children, Shlomo, Aliza Malya, Ezra Meshulam, Menachem, Shira Fradel, and Devora: You bring much joy and meaning to my life. Thank you for being so excited about this book. May we continue to be a source of *nachas* for each other.

Introduction

WHEN MOSHE RABBEINU is asked by Hashem to confront Pharaoh and redeem Am Yisrael from their enslavement in Egypt, Moshe demurs because of his inability to speak clearly: "I am not a man of words…for I am heavy of mouth and heavy of speech."[1] Yet, forty years later, Moshe delivers one of the greatest speeches ever given, as recorded in *Sefer Devarim*: "And these are the words that Moshe spoke to all of Israel, on the other side of the Jordan…"[2] The midrash attributes the dramatic change in Moshe to the healing effects of the Torah's language:

> *See how beloved the language of Torah is, as it cures the tongue. Moshe, until he was privileged to receive the Torah, it is written about him, "I am not a man of words," but once he was privileged to receive the Torah, his tongue was cured and he began speaking words.*[3]

What emerges from this midrash is that the Torah doesn't intend to merely prescribe and proscribe certain actions, but to provide us with a language with which to make sense of the world and communicate that understanding to others.

Language doesn't only *reflect* our thinking; language *affects* our thinking. For example, a euphemism, a vague word substituted for one considered too harsh or direct, doesn't just sound less offensive to the ear; it has the power to reshape the way we think (and therefore feel)

---

1 *Shemos* 4:10.
2 *Devarim* 1:1.
3 *Devarim Rabbah* 1:1.

about the experience. What once was deemed negative is, by way of a euphemism, redefined as a different and, thus, acceptable experience. An employer sleeps more easily when, instead of "firing" his employee, he is "downsizing." A consumer is more confident about her purchase when she buys a "certified pre-owned" car, rather than a "used" car.

Precisely because the words we use affect the way we think, reformers are known to appropriate morally pregnant words to validate their cause. Once the link between the phrase "human dignity" and a given cause is solidified in the public mind, there is almost no way to assail the cause anymore; doing so is no longer an attack on the cause, but one on "human dignity." No one wants to be an enemy of "human dignity." Likewise, nobody would side with the "oppressor" against the "victim." Who decides, however, who is the "victim" and who is the "oppressor"? Once it is determined, though, and a given narrative is created and accepted, the thoughts and emotions of multitudes are forever altered. The power of language to affect human behavior cannot be denied.

Because the Torah is comprehensive and touches upon every facet of the human experience, the student of the Torah has an alternative language with which to analyze and apprehend any and every issue that arises, and articulate his understanding to others. The Torah, replete with expressive words and precise terminology, enables us to confront the world with a narrative of our own.

The rabbi, therefore, is in a unique position to influence his congregants and students. When faced with current events or personal issues, there are many languages an individual can utilize to make sense of them. Newspapers, magazines, books, theatre, television, movies, etc., all provide an individual with various words to think in. More often than not, however, congregants and students will turn to the Torah for answers and explanations. Sometimes, they confront our sacred texts directly. At other times, they turn to their rabbi to give them a vocabulary and categories of thought with which to navigate life's challenges.

This book is a result of those encounters. Week after week, year after year, we are faced with complex and confusing situations and events. With the help of Hashem, I have tried, over these past five and a half years, to provide the members and *mispallelim* of Young Israel of Avenue J not answers, but a language with which to analyze and discuss life's vicissitudes and vexing issues.

This book intends to expose its readers to new dimensions of the Torah's vibrant language and to provoke thought and conversation beyond its pages. At least, it has enriched my vocabulary and has helped me make more sense of our complicated world. With obvious differences, like Moshe Rabbeinu, I have ended this journey of composition more articulate than when I began.

Bereishis

A Threat to Parenthood

WHEN HASHEM FIRST introduces Adam HaRishon to his wife, Adam instantly recognizes their compatibility and names her accordingly: "And the man said, 'This is now bone of my bones, and flesh of my flesh; she shall be called Woman, because she was taken out of Man.'"[1] This name, however, is short-lived. Immediately after Hashem pronounces the consequences for all those involved in partaking of the forbidden fruit of the *Eitz HaDaas*, Adam renames his wife: "And Adam called his wife's name Chavah; because she was the mother of all life."[2] Why does Adam decide to give his wife this particular name at precisely this moment, and not earlier? From her inception, she was destined to be

---

1 *Bereishis* 2:23. The Hebrew word for woman, *"ishah,"* is linguistically derived from the Hebrew word for man, *"ish."*
2 *Bereishis* 3:20.

"the mother of all life," as Hashem had enjoined the two of them to be "fruitful and multiply."[3] What changed?

Rashi, because of this difficulty, invokes the principle that "there is no chronological order in the Torah."[4] For stylistic and exegetical purposes, says *Rashi*, the Torah interrupts its discussion of how Adam gave names to all living creatures, including his wife, with the narrative of the snake and the forbidden fruit. Once the Torah completes that episode, it returns to where it left off, with Adam giving out names.[5]

However, if we are to assume that, despite the abovementioned principle, the Torah does present these events in chronological order,[6] what emerges is that their sin and its consequences inspire Adam to rename his wife "Chavah." Why?

Often, when an idea or institution is threatened and needs to be kept alive, a new word or phrase is coined by its defenders to preserve the idea's salience and relevance. As Rabbi Jonathan Sacks says:

> *Words are often born when the phenomenon they name is under threat. The adjective "orthodox" first appeared in a Jewish context in France in the early nineteenth century in the course of the debate about Jewish citizenship in the new nation-state. For the first time in the modern world the traditional terms of Jewish existence were thrown into question. Alternatives were proposed. Some argued that Judaism must change. Those who disagreed were given the label "orthodox." Only when something is challenged does it need a name. Until then it is taken for granted, part of the background.*[7]

---

3   *Bereishis* 1:28.
4   TB *Pesachim* 6b.
5   Commentary to *Bereishis* 3:20.
6   Unlike *Rashi* who applies the principle freely throughout his commentary (for some other examples see *Bereishis* 6:3, *Shemos* 31:18, and *Vayikra* 8:2), the *Ramban* limits the principle exclusively to where the Torah itself specifies that an event took place on an earlier date (see his commentary to *Vayikra* 16:1 and *Bamidbar* 16:1).
7   Jonathan Sacks, *Future Tense: Jews, Judaism, and Israel in the Twenty-First Century* (Schocken Books, 2009), p. 25.

In any given culture, when an idea, attitude, or habit is a matter-of-fact, when it is unremarkable and goes unnoticed because it is almost as familiar as the air we breathe, there is no need for language to justify its existence. Only when something is no longer a given, only when its goodness or right to exist is questioned, are words required to defend it.

With this insight in mind, we can better appreciate Chavah's name change. As a punishment for eating from the *Eitz HaDaas* and for enticing her husband to eat as well, she is informed by Hashem: "I will greatly multiply your pain and your travail; in pain you shall bear children."[8] Because of her sin, giving birth would cease to be a casual, painless, and completely harmless process. Instead, it would be difficult, painful, and dangerous. As a result, woman's role as mother of children came into question. Because of the devastating decree, it was no longer clear whether she would willingly subject herself to the torment of childbearing and tolerate the physical, emotional, and psychological burdens of pregnancy and labor. Before their sin, motherhood — childbearing and childrearing — was taken for granted, a given in their lives; it therefore needed no name. All of a sudden, however, in the wake of their sin, the idea of motherhood came under threat.

So Adam HaRishon, fearing that his wife would delay or even opt out entirely from motherhood, creates a new word, *chavah*, which means "mother of all life," to defend the majesty of motherhood and justify its ordeal. By adorning his wife with the new name Chavah, Adam accentuates her dignity.

In the Western world, birth rates are plummeting. Although it is usually assumed that economic pressures, such as financial instability and insecurity, cause birth rates to decline, often the opposite is true. Even in an affluent society birth rates will drop if another condition is satisfied: secularization. When the traditional, religious values of restraint, self-sacrifice, and deferred gratification are supplanted by the

---

8   *Bereishis* 3:16.

creed of unbridled self-indulgence, excess, and instant gratification in a wealthy society capable of accommodating these appetites, parenthood comes under threat.

Because economic prosperity in a secular society induces low fertility, Andrew Oswald, a professor at the University of Warwick who studies the relationship between economics and happiness, predicts that many families will continue to shrink. "I love my own daughter to bits. But skiing and sports cars without baby seats can be fun too," he says. "That's why only-children are the secular trend of a rich society we've been moving toward for the past one hundred years."[9] In the past, the pain and dangers of childbearing, as well as financial concerns, served as deterrents to parenthood. Today, in an affluent society that enjoys the benefits of modern medicine, these deterrents have been replaced with the ever-increasing desire for more money, more leisure, and more instant gratification.

The Torah records that in the times of Enosh, Adam's grandson: "It was then that man began to proclaim in the Name of Hashem."[10] Ostensibly, the Torah's intention is to present the root cause behind the degeneration of mankind, which ultimately warrants the coming of the Flood. Still, the issue is not clear. Where is the indecency in "proclaiming in the Name of Hashem"? Isn't it a respectable and commendable practice, worthy of praise? Why is it condemned?

Rav Shimshon Raphael Hirsch explains in the name of his teacher, Chacham Isaac Bernays, that in the days of Enosh, because the awareness of Hashem was rapidly declining, a need arose "to proclaim in the Name of Hashem." To preclude monotheism from becoming a thing of the past, from heading into the dustbin of history, a concerted effort was made by Hashem's few remaining adherents to pronounce and publicize His Name among the masses. Unfortunately, their efforts did not achieve their objective.

---

9   Lauren Sandler, "The Only Child: Debunking the Myths," *Time* magazine, July 2010.
10   *Bereishis* 4:26.

Rav Shimshon Raphael Hirsch concludes his analysis of the generation of Enosh by observing that the degeneration of society ultimately paves the way for the Jewish people and its destiny:

> *The need "to proclaim the Name of G-d" is the gateway to the history of the Jewish people, who are to awaken the hearts of all men to the awareness of man's true calling and of man's relationship to G-d. Toward this end, the people of Israel is chosen, whose mission is none other than "to proclaim in the Name of G-d."*[11]

Parenthood presupposes an ethic of sacrifice, commitment, and deferred gratification. A society that does not embrace parenthood betrays its moral decline. The dominant culture of Western society is increasingly becoming more secular, and as a result, parenthood is no longer taken for granted as a fact of life.

It is our responsibility to ensure that Torah values and virtues remain alive and abiding in the cultures we live in. In order to "awaken the hearts of all men to the awareness of man's true calling and man's relationship to Hashem," our chosen lifestyles should proclaim not only the Name of Hashem, but also the name Chavah!

---

11   Commentary to *Bereishis* 4:26.

Hevel's Approach to Life's Brevity

AFTER ADAM AND Chavah are banished from Gan Eden, Chavah conceives, gives birth to a boy, and names him Kayin, for "I have acquired a man with Hashem."[1] Soon after, she gives birth to Kayin's brother, Hevel. What is striking is that the Torah only records Chavah's inspiration for her first son's name. When Hevel is born, we are given no insight behind his name. Perhaps Chavah never articulates her reason for the choice of the name Hevel. Why not? Why the sudden reticence?

Troubled by Chavah's silence when she names Hevel, the *Ramban* offers the following explanation:

> *She called the first one by a name associated with "acquisition," and the second "Hevel" because all the acquisitions and achievements of man are as fleeting as mist (hevel). And she did not want — she could not bring herself — to express this sentiment; therefore, no reason is given for the second name.*[2]

Chavah's newly acquired awareness of her mortality haunts her. All of her achievements — past, present, and future — are tainted by undertones of despondency and a sense of futility. Interestingly, Chavah's attitude toward life sounds familiar.

"Vanity of vanities," says Koheles, "vanity of vanities. All is vanity (*hevel*)."[3] The word *hevel* — which is the leitmotif of *Sefer Koheles* — is usually translated as "vain," carrying with it negative connotations

---

1   Bereishis 4:1.
2   Commentary to ibid.
3   Koheles 1:2.

that life is futile and meaningless. The *Ramban*, who translates *hevel* as "fleeting mist," however, shifts the focus of the book from futility to transience. From this perspective, the question Koheles seeks to answer is how to confront the fleetingness of our existence. Based on the Ramban's interpretation, some have suggested that the wisdom Koheles ultimately bequeaths to his audience is this: transience as *inspiration*. Instead of disillusionment, an acute awareness of life's fleetingness can give birth to a sense of *urgency*.

To be sure, Koheles is initially disillusioned by the transience of life, causing him to see all that there is and all that man achieves as futile. "And I hated life, for all is mere breath (*hevel*) and herding the wind. And I hated all things got from my toil that I had toiled under the sun, that I should leave it to the man who will come after me."[4] But Koheles doesn't stop there; he has only begun his existential journey.

Throughout the book, Koheles works through the implications of life's transience, and progresses from dejection and disappointment to acceptance and appreciation and, finally, to joy and inspiration. For example, Koheles enjoins his reader to: "Enjoy life with a woman whom you love all your days of mere breath that have been given to you under the sun."[5] Then he urges his reader, "All that your hand manages to do with your strength, do, for there is no doing nor reckoning nor knowledge nor wisdom in She'ol where you are going."[6] Life is a gift, implores Koheles. Don't squander it. Do something with it.

The *Ramban*'s connection between the name Hevel and the fleetingness of man's life has led some to posit that Koheles, when he organized his musings with the word *hevel*, was influenced by the story of Kayin and Hevel. Perhaps we can suggest that the respective attitudes of Kayin and Hevel correspond to the beginning and end of Koheles's philosophical journey.

---

4   Ibid. 2:17.
5   Ibid. 9:9.
6   Ibid. 9:10.

Chavah, as revealed by the *Ramban*, exemplifies Koheles's initial stance toward the transience of life. Not surprisingly, her disillusionment is shared by her eldest son, Kayin. It is the subtext of all his actions.

- Kayin brings an unexceptional and uninspired offering; whatever kind of fruits he happens to chance upon, irrespective of their quality, he brings as a gift to Hashem.
- Moreover, he doesn't bring an offering from the "fruit of *his* land." Kayin offers "fruit of *the* land."[7]

Undoubtedly, Kayin brings fruit from land that he owns, but that is not how he perceives it. The shadow of his inevitable death, the fleetingness of his existence, prevents him from experiencing the land as "his" and from fully enjoying his material wealth and success, what has been given him under the sun. Trapped by the transience of life, Kayin, like his mother, lives an uninspired, unfulfilled, and joyless life.

But not Hevel.

Hevel, perhaps somewhat distanced from his mother's attitude by dint of birth order, confronts life's fleetingness differently. Instead of being depressed by life's transience, Hevel is inspired by it. Animated by a sense of urgency, Hevel lives life to its fullest. He takes advantage of all that life has to offer, appreciating and enjoying all that has been given to him under the sun: Hevel's offering is brought from the "best"[8] of "*his* flock."[9]

Having his transient life shortened prematurely, Hevel does not leave any biological offspring. However, he did leave a legacy: we can all be Hevel's spiritual heirs.

May we all live inspired, joyous, and fulfilled lives — lives marked by a sense of urgency.

---

7   *Bereishis* 4:3.
8   Ibid. 4:4.
9   Ibid.

Noach

The Perils of Caretaking

IN THE EARLY 1900s, the average life expectancy in the United States of America was age forty. One hundred years later, due to advancements in medicine and technology, Americans are now reaching their twilight years in their eighties and even nineties. With more and more octogenarians and nonagenarians among the population, the demographics of the country are drastically changing. It is projected that by the year 2035, the number of Americans over eighty-five years old will have more than doubled from about five million to 11.5 million.

Interestingly, as society's most aged segment continues to grow, another population has become salient: the caretaker. Not only are geriatric nurses and home-care aides more visible in our communities, but family members have increasingly assumed the primary responsibility of caring for their loved ones whose bodies and minds often fail them. As if the regular stresses of life weren't enough, these caretakers have to cope with the additional emotional burden and physical toll that come with caretaking. How best to manage and navigate the inner conflicts and external demands that are thrust upon a caretaker is not easily articulated, but the realization that we are not alone in our struggle often makes things easier. In fact, although it seems that caretaking and its concomitant challenges is a nascent issue, the caretaker is not a new phenomenon, but dates back to the beginning of time, to antediluvian times; as far back as Noach.

During the Flood, everything on dry land ceased to exist. From man to animals to birds, nothing remained — with the exception, of course, of one person and those under his stewardship. As the Torah records, "Only (*ach*) Noach survived, and those with him in the ark."[1] *Rashi* provides three explanations for the word *ach*, each of which reflects the word's connotation of exclusion or minimization:

1. Its simple meaning: alone. Relative to everyone and everything else, Noach alone remained alive.
2. The word intimates that on the ark Noach was coughing and vomiting blood. The word *ach* — a word phonetically similar to the sound one makes when coughing and retching — conveys that Noach's health was compromised from the overexertion of caring for all the animals.
3. The word alludes to an injury suffered by Noach on the ark. Because he once delayed giving food to the lion, the lion attacked and wounded him, crippling him for life.[2]

What is startling is *Rashi*'s need to give not one, not two, but three different interpretations for the word *ach*. What compels him to do this? Are they somehow related and therefore indispensable to one another? Moreover, the lion's reaction is striking in its cruelty. Noach dedicates himself to care for the lion, sacrificing his own well-being in the process, and because he tarries one time the lion lashes out. How could the lion be so unreasonable, so unforgiving?

---

1   *Bereishis* 7:23.
2   Commentary to ibid.

To resolve these difficulties, we can suggest that Noach can be seen as a metaphor for those who assume the care of a loved one who has fallen terribly ill or has been devastated by the effects of advanced aging. Although caring for a loved one can be a transformative experience, there is no denying the difficulties involved. The three *ach*'s of Noach, taken together, represent three facets of the hardship incurred by the caretaker:

1. Unlike the demands of parenting or a career, which are many but mostly scheduled and anticipated, the caretaker's life is replete with unexpected emergencies, such as a sudden fall or a pulled-out feeding tube, that consistently disrupt one's regular daily routine. Consequently, it becomes a challenge for the caretaker to keep appointments and to socialize. Often, the caretaker becomes as socially isolated as the elderly patient no longer capable of interaction. To make matters worse, when one's lifelong partner or cherished parent loses the ability to communicate in any meaningful way, the silence and loneliness can be unbearable. The caretaker experiences what psychologists call ambiguous loss, the emptiness felt when a loved one is present, yet absent. And the most tragic part of caretaking — what sets it starkly apart from parenting and its expectation of growth and joy — is that, in the end, after all the sacrifice and investment, the caretaker is left bereft. Having once had to adjust to the challenges of caretaking, the caretaker now has to adapt and reorient himself to life without his loved one. *Only (ach) Noach remained.*
2. The adverse effects of caring for a loved one are not only social and emotional, but physical, as well. Being the primary caretaker of a loved one takes its toll on the body. The caretaker can become worn down, even to the point of illness. It is important that the caretaker be mindful of this outcome and make accommodations for self-care, whereby he finds time to relax and enjoy himself — guilt-free. Extended family and friends also play a crucial role throughout the process. Aware of the caretaker's

grueling schedule and abiding responsibilities, the reprieve others can offer the caretaker can be invaluable, as their involvement can determine the caretaker's quality of health. *Only (ach) — the physically compromised — Noach remained.*

3. Without downplaying it in any way, the death of our loved ones may not be the most emotionally difficult part of the caretaking experience. Due to certain illnesses and the effects of advanced aging, our loved ones change. Alas, in our care, they become irritable, irrational, unforgiving, and even ferocious. They can lash out like a lion, saying terrible things that wound and scar, never to be healed. What's more, our mothers we cherish, our fathers we adore, our spouses whom we've shared a life together, somehow forget everything, including our names. After all we've given and sacrificed, they can't even remember who we are. It's all so cruel. *Only (ach) Noach remained.*

The Torah, though, does try to offer solace to the burdened or bereft caretaker. After the Flood reaches its climax, we read: "And G-d remembered Noah and all the beasts and all the cattle that were with him in the ark, and G-d caused a spirit to pass over the earth, and the waters subsided."[3] What is the nature of the spirit that envelops the world? *Rashi* explains that "a spirit of consolation and relief passed before Him."[4]

Hashem remembers the caretaker.

He remembers the caretaker's energy, effort, and empathy.

He remembers the caretaker's love, ailing, and loss.

As a result, Hashem touches the caretaker with His spirit, a spirit of comfort and relief.

---

3   *Bereishis* 8:1.
4   Commentary to ibid.

Noach and the Wonderful Wizard of Oz

IN HIS INTRODUCTION to *The Wonderful Wizard of Oz*, L. Frank Baum candidly offers his impetus for writing the book. He laments how the "old-time fairy tale" has become a thing of the past, supplanted by "wonder tales," which are less entertaining and enjoyable for children, since they have been written less by the desire to please children than the drive "to point a fearsome moral to each tale." Baum asserts that, contrary to this popular trend, his latest children's tale "was written solely to please children of today."[1] Baum, though, was just setting his audience up. *The Wonderful Wizard of Oz* — while remaining faithful to its professed aim to delight and bring joy to children — is pregnant with symbolism, hidden meaning, and moral lessons. By highlighting one such lesson in this delightful tale, we can better appreciate the personality of Noach.

When reading the story about the Flood, one is so distracted by Noach's devotion and preoccupation with the construction of the ark and the subsequent sequestering of himself, his family, and animals inside that one tends to gloss over the fact that Noach, during this entire time, does not concern himself with anything else. As far as we know, not once does Noach daven to Hashem to reconsider. Not once does he respectfully, but forcefully, protest before Hashem on behalf of the people of his generation.[2] Not once do we find that Noach actively

---

[1] L. Frank Baum, introduction to *The Wonderful Wizard of Oz* (Barnes & Noble Classics, 2005).
[2] Contrast Noach's silence with Avraham Avinu's lengthy stance in defense of the people of Sodom, see *Bereishis* 18:23–32.

engages his fellow citizens in an attempt to influence them favorably and persuade them to change. Instead, Noach does the opposite: he disengages from society[3] and intentionally delays bearing offspring lest they be adversely affected by the decadence and decay around them.[4] For five hundred years, instead of populating the earth with his own kin and kind, instead of starting a counterculture movement embodying morality, decency, virtue, justice, and righteousness, Noach remains barren — barren of progeny, ideas, and initiative. And because of his passivity and inaction, Hashem ultimately holds Noach responsible for the Flood, referring to it as, "the waters of Noach."[5]

Noach, it seems, exemplifies the personality our sages refer to as a "righteous man who is not good."[6] "Righteous" because he is good to Heaven; "not good" because he is not good to man. Rav Aharon Lichtenstein, however, cannot countenance the idea that an individual who is a murderer, thief, or liar — not good to man — would be considered a "righteous" individual, on any level. Instead, the type of person our sages are describing, says Rav Lichtenstein is:

> *Not a person who tramples underfoot the whole area of bein adam l'chaveiro [laws between man and his fellow man], but a person who is simply oblivious to it. He pours his energies into and concentrates upon the area of bein adam l'Makom [laws between man and G-d], to such an extent that he has neither the energy, resources, nor motivation to work within the area of bein adam l'chaveiro as well. It is in this sense that he is evil to mankind. He does nothing for them. He has no social conscience and is insensitive to the needs of others. He is totally concerned with the area of being good to Heaven.*[7]

---

3   *Zohar* I:58b (Pitzker edition, 2004).
4   *Tanchuma Bereishis* 39, *Bereishis Rabbah* 26:2, and *Bamidbar Rabbah* 14:12.
5   *Yeshayahu* 54:9.
6   BT *Kiddushin* 40a.
7   Aharon Lichtenstein, *By His Light: Character & Values in the Service of G-d* (Ktav, 2003), p. 116.

What still needs to be explored is the psyche of Noach, of the righteous man who is not good. What motivates such a person to engage in devotional piety to the extent that he has nothing left for mankind? Why is it that Noach has neither "the energy, resources, nor motivation" to be conscious of and engage his fellow man? What are the theological and psychological underpinnings of his personality that inhibit Noach from taking social action?

For some insight into the peculiar personality of the "righteous man who is not good," we follow Dorothy into the Land of Oz. After the tornado sweeps her up from the dreary plains of Kansas and drops her in the brightly colored Oz, Dorothy sets out on a long and difficult journey in search of the wizard, Oz, whom Dorothy believes will be able to send her back home. It probably comes as no surprise to you that, along the way, Dorothy meets and befriends the Scarecrow, the Tin Man, and the Lion. They, too, could benefit from having an audience with the great wizard, since only he has the power to grant them what they lack and so desperately want: The Scarecrow professes to have no brains at all, the Tin Man asserts that he has no heart, and the Lion avows that he lacks courage.

No sooner than we meet this motley crew do we discover that everything is not what it seems:

- The Tin Man, who purports to be incapable of love due to his lack of a heart, is the most emotional, sensitive, and compassionate of the bunch.
- The Scarecrow, who repeatedly affirms that he lacks any intelligence whatsoever, as a result of having no brains, is the most ingenious of them all. It is the Scarecrow's quick and creative thinking that saves the group from failure or certain death, time and time again.
- The self-professed "cowardly Lion" is as courageous and fearless in the face of danger as one would expect the King of the Jungle to be.

When they finally arrive in the Emerald City, since the Great Oz will only see them one at a time, Dorothy enters his chamber alone and sees an enormous Head sitting on a big throne laid in emeralds. As Dorothy gazes at the Head in wonder and fear, the Head opens its mouth and speaks:

> "I am Oz, the Great and Terrible. Who are you, and why do you seek me?"
>
> "I am Dorothy, the Small and Meek. I have come to you for help."[8]

Yes, of course: "Dorothy, the Small and Meek." Dorothy, who set out to travel alone and on foot in a foreign land in search of a way home, who rescued the helpless Scarecrow from atop his pole, who discovered and saved the forsaken Tin Man, who confronted a lion (the Lion), and who led a motley crew of strangers on an epic journey. Dorothy, the Small and Meek!

At this point, what should become obvious to the reader is that Dorothy and her companions are all inherently capable — they all possess and exhibit the talents and resources they profess to lack. The only problem is: they do not believe in themselves. And as many of you already know, the greatest irony of the tale is that, all along, Dorothy has the ability to return home to Kansas all on her own. She simply doesn't believe in herself.

Why not?

Baum, writing in America at the turn of the twentieth century, influenced by the rising tide of agnosticism, on the one hand, and the growing skepticism of organized religion, on the other, attributed the self-doubt to religious piety and devotion. Living in a Christian-dominated America that he found to be backward and primitive, Baum (like many freethinkers of his time[9]) perceived that the church's demand for blind obedience and a fixation with a transcendent world engendered feelings of inadequacy, dependency, and self-negation.

---

8   L. Frank Baum, *The Wonderful Wizard of Oz* (Barnes & Noble Classics, 2005), p. 106.
9   Susan Jacoby, *Free Thinkers: A History of American Secularism* (Henry Holt and Co., 2004), p. 11.

The religious personality who totally submits to G-d and obsesses about the next world enters a vicious cycle of insecurity and timidity. The more he depends on G-d's grace for assistance, and sees this world as unredeemable, the more insecure and uncertain of his ability to navigate this world he becomes. In turn, he seeks more security in G-d and comfort in the promise of the next world, which begets even more insecurity about this world, and so on.

Standing in the venerable presence of the Great and Powerful Oz (G-d), in the faraway, majestic City of Emeralds (a transcendent reality), Dorothy (the devout Christian) experiences herself as small, meek, and helpless. This is the essence of the religious personality, according to Baum.[10]

Almost a half a century later, Rav Soloveitchik produced *Halachik Man* to disabuse people of this widespread notion that the religious personality often encountered is the only type there is. Indeed, the religious personality who is characterized by fear and a lack of a sense of agency due to his submission to G-d and preoccupation with the next world (who Rav Soloveitchik referred to as *homo religiosus*) is far from ideal.[11]

There is a different, more authentic type of religious personality: *halachik man*. Unlike *homo religiosus*, *halachik man* is confident, creative, independent, and assertive. *Halachik man* yearns not for some other, distant world, but to create the ideal human society in this world. Wherever *halachik man* turns, he sees opportunity for refinement. He envisions a culture shaped and imprinted with the values and constructs of the Torah. Instead of being diminished by his faith, *halachik man* is ennobled and animated by his faith in Hashem and His Torah.[12]

Noach, the sages tell us, lacked faith. Noach, as we are told, enters the ark "because of the waters of the flood."[13] According to Rabbi

---

10 Michael Patrick Hearn, *The Annotated Wizard of Oz* (W. W. Norton & Company, 2000), p. xciv. Katherine M. Rogers, *L. Frank Baum: Creator of Oz* (De Capo Press, 2002) p.33.
11 Joseph B. Soloveitchik, *Halakhic Man* (The Jewish Publication Society, 1983) pp. 40–5, 74.
12 Joseph B. Soloveitchik, *Halakhic Man* (The Jewish Publication Society, 1983) pp. 40–5, 71–2, 94–5, 99–101.
13 *Bereishis* 7:7.

Yochanan, Noach "was lacking in genuine faith, for had the water not actually reached his ankles, he would never have gotten into the ark."[14] Classically understood, this teaching conveys that Noach, all along, doesn't fully believe that Hashem will actually bring a flood. Not until the waters reach his ankles does Noach realize that Hashem is true to His word. The *Kedushas Levi*, Rabbi Levi Yitzchak of Berditchev, however, offers an alternative, penetrating insight. He posits that Noach had perfect faith in Hashem; the problem was that Noach lacked genuine faith in himself. According to the *Kedushas Levi*:

> *One of the reasons that he did not daven for his fellow man may have been that he felt inadequate to be able to cancel a decree that Hashem had told him He had issued...he did not consider himself as especially righteous.*[15]

This insight into Noach's psyche is, perhaps, the meaning behind the famous dispute between our sages as to whether Noah's righteousness was absolute or only relative:

> *There are those who expound this phrase [righteous...in his generations] for praise. Resh Lakish maintained: Even in his generations he was righteous — how much more so in other generations.*
>
> *And there are those who expound it disparagingly. Rav Yochanan said: In his generations he was considered righteous, but not in other generations.*[16]

At first glance, it is troubling that our sages would argue over a historical fact, whether or not Noach's righteousness was absolute. To be sure, the Gemara is a collection of wide-ranging disputes, and our tradition maintains that each position expressed and presented is representative of the truth. However, this multiple-truth doctrine,

---

14   *Bereishis Rabbah* 32:6.
15   *Kedushas Levi*, trans. Eliyahu Munk (Judaica Press, 2009), pp. 28–9.
16   BT *Sanhedrin* 108a and *Bereishis Rabbah* 30:9.

seemingly, is only understandable in the realm of law and philosophy: each position views the issue from a certain perspective, neither one addressing the issue comprehensively, from all sides. Or, the disputants are arguing about definitions and classifications, each one emphasizing one characteristic over another, not unlike what scientists do. However, to encounter an argument concerning an historical fact is troubling. Was Noach an absolute "righteous man" or not? How can both views be true?

Based on the *Kedushas Levi*'s insight, it follows that the two opinions do not necessarily disagree about the fact of Noach's righteousness. Both agree that Noach was an absolute *tzaddik*. Rather, the "dissenting" opinion is assuming a different perspective: If you were to ask Noach what he thought of himself, what would he say? If you were to ask Noach if he saw his righteousness as absolute or only as relative to his generation, how would Noach respond? The answer, sadly, is that Noach would have said that his righteousness was only relative. Noach, himself, tragically interprets Hashem's acclamation disparagingly.

Where do we see this? Noach neither davens for his fellow citizens nor engages them in any significant way because he feels inadequate and incapable of affecting change. What Noach perceives as religion's demand for blind faith and total obedience strips him of the psychological resources necessary to take initiative and be assertive. The culture of obedience and preoccupation with other realms of existence that is characteristic of many religious doctrines inhibits Noach from feeling responsible and fully participating in society as a creative force. In the end, all Noach is capable of doing is preserving and protecting what is ever left of a once noble and decent society.

Can we identify with Noach? As Hashem does to Noach, He praises us, "It is you I have seen to be righteous before Me in this generation." However, do we view ourselves as praiseworthy? On an individual and collective level, do we believe in ourselves and our ability to impact the world? Do we have the sense of responsibility, the confidence, and the courage necessary to effect change?

Let us learn from Noach's tragic mistake and interpret Hashem's praise of us as words of encouragement. By doing so, we avoid limiting ourselves to the humble task of preserving and protecting what we have left, and, instead, we open up ourselves to our noble calling to create, to shape, and to lead.

A Second Chance

FORTY DAYS AFTER the ark comes to rest upon the mountains of Ararat, Noach opens a portal in the ark and sends out the raven. The raven, however, does not fly off in search of a nesting area; instead, it encircles the ark endlessly until dry land appears. Our sages, in an attempt to explain this peculiar behavior, imagine the following dialogue between the raven and Noach:

> Said Reish Lakish: The raven put forward an irrefutable argument to Noach. It said to him: "Your Master hates me and you hate me. Your Master hates me, for He commanded, 'Of every pure animal take seven pairs, but from the animal that is not pure take only a pair.' And you hate me, for you resist taking from the species that has seven pairs of its kind and instead send out from a species that only has two of its kind remaining. If something were to happen to me on my journey, would the world not lack one of its creatures? Or, maybe this is exactly what you intend, for you are interested in my spouse!"[1]

Could the raven have been more ungrateful and obnoxious? However, in truth, what did Noach expect? The raven, after all, is notorious for its callousness and cruelty. It doesn't even care for its own young; as a result, Hashem Himself must tend to them. That is why Hashem is referred to as the One "Who prepares for the raven its nourishment, when its young cry to G-d and wander about without food."[2] And it is

---

1 BT *Sanhedrin* 108b.
2 *Iyov* 38:41.

Hashem, not the raven, who responds to their pangs of hunger, as it says, "He gives food to the animals and feeds the young ravens when they cry."³ Why, then, did Noach choose, from all the birds at hand, the raven to survey the land?

The *Ohr HaChaim Hakadosh*, troubled by this difficulty, is compelled to reread the *pesukim*. The question assumes that Noach sends the raven on a reconnaissance mission. Not so, says the *Ohr HaChaim*. The raven isn't sent on a mission; it is driven away.⁴

Why? Based on a close reading of the text, our sages infer that while in the ark, intimate relations were prohibited for everyone, man and creature alike. When Noach is commanded to enter the ark, he is grouped with his sons, while his wife is grouped with his daughters-in-law. But when they are enjoined to leave the ark, Noach is paired with his wife, as his sons are paired with their respective wives. The initial separation as they embark, contrasted with the later coupling as they exit, indicates that only after they emerged from the ark would they be able to resume intimacy.⁵

But not everyone adheres to this norm. The raven, says the Gemara, characteristically disregards protocol and continues to be intimate with its spouse. Aware of the raven's audacity and breach of convention, Noach banishes him from the ark the first chance he gets.⁶ This reading is borne out in the text: In contrast to when Noach sends out the raven for an unspecified task, when Noach sends the dove, he does so, "to see whether the waters subsided."⁷

Perhaps, however, we can suggest a different answer, one that assumes that Noach indeed sends the raven — the cruelest of all creatures — on a fact-finding mission.

In his introduction to *Men Are from Mars, Women Are from Venus*, John Gray shares with his readers a personal transformative moment

---

3   *Tehillim* 147:9.
4   Commentary to *Bereishis* 8:7.
5   BT *Sanhedrin* 108b.
6   Ibid.
7   *Ohr HaChaim* in his Commentary to *Bereishis* 8:7-8.

that saved his second marriage and, ultimately, became the basis of his best-seller book that has helped millions of people. Soon after his wife Bonnie gave birth to their daughter, John came home from work one day to find his wife suffering in pain. Her painkillers had run out and she had been forced to endure the pain all day long. Bonnie was miserable and lonely, and felt that nobody cared. John became defensive and frustrated, wondering out loud why she hadn't contacted him at work for help. As his temper began to flare, John turned around and reached for the front door. Then, John recalls, something happened that would change his life.

> *Bonnie said, "Stop, please don't leave. This is when I need you the most. I'm in pain. I haven't slept in days. Please listen to me."*
>
> *I stopped for a moment to listen. She said, "John Gray, you're a fair-weather friend! As long as I'm sweet, loving Bonnie you are here for me, but as soon as I'm not, you walk right out that door."*
>
> *Then she paused, and her eyes filled with tears. As her tone shifted she said, "Right now I'm in pain. I have nothing to give, this is when I need you the most. Please, come over here and hold me. You don't have to say anything. I just need to feel your arms around me. Please don't go.*
>
> *I walked over and silently held her. She wept in my arms. After a few minutes, she thanked me for not leaving. She told me she just needed to feel me holding her...*
>
> *That day, for the first time, I didn't leave her. I stayed, and it felt great. I succeeded in giving to her when she really needed me...I marveled at how easy it was for me to support her when I was shown the way. How had I missed this? She just needed me to go over and hold her...*
>
> *In my previous relationships, I had become indifferent and unloving at difficult times, simply because I didn't know what*

> else to do. As a result, my first marriage had been very painful and difficult. This incident with Bonnie revealed to me how I could change this pattern.[8]

Despite his previous history, despite his tendencies and entrenched patterns of behavior (all of which helped to undermine his first marriage), John Gray was able to take advantage of a second opportunity and change. To be sure, he needed someone to show him the way, to educate him. Once enlightened, John seized the moment and took off.

Perhaps Noach selects the raven for the all-important mission precisely because the raven had previously exhibited callous and cruel tendencies. But that was before. Before the ark. Before the Flood. Before everything living outside the ark was destroyed and wiped away. When Noach opens the portal of the ark, he opens it into a new world, where a fresh start and endless possibilities beckon. Noach chooses the raven, as if to say to it, "You get a fresh start, too. Despite the past, you can change your pattern of behavior. From here on, the raven can be known as a caring, concerned, compassionate creature! You have it within you. And I can be your guide. Look at what I've accomplished on the ark. I can show you the way."

Sadly, the raven dismisses Noach's offer. It assumes its old habits, unwilling to change. Given a second chance, the raven fails.

Still, the raven's story isn't over. As alluded to in the text here,[9] Eliyahu HaNavi, during a drought and while in hiding, is supported by the ravens. "The ravens would bring him bread and meat in the morning and bread and meat in the evening."[10] *Metzudos David* explains that Hashem purposefully sends the ravens, known for their callousness and cruelty, to assist Eliyahu, as if to say to the acerbic and zealous prophet, "Look, even the ravens can be moved to care, even they have the capacity for

---

8   John Gray, *Men Are from Mars, Women Are from Venus* (Quill, 2004), pp. xxv–xxvii.
9   *Bereishis* 8:7. As *Rashi* comments, the raven's encircling of the ark "until the waters dried from upon the earth," foreshadows its mission during the drought in the days of Eliyahu HaNavi.
10 *I Melachim* 17:6.

compassion. How can you, Eliyahu, not show more compassion for the people of Israel.[11] Eliyahu, you have it in you, you have the capacity to change. I can be your guide. For I, the G-d of vengeance, am also merciful and compassionate. I can show you how to balance the two traits, allowing for compassion without compromising on your acute sense of right and wrong."

Like the raven, John Gray, and Eliyahu HaNavi, we have all formed habits of thought and patterns of behavior. Most of them are positive. Some of them, however, are undesirable, and cause harm to others and ourselves. Wouldn't it be great if we would change those patterns? To be sure, to change is hard. There is a reason the raven fails. There are many psychological, emotional, and social obstacles that often need to be overcome on the road to change. But life is full of second chances. Our past patterns do not have to determine our present choices. The next time we find ourselves looking through a portal at a brand-new world, let us learn a lesson from the raven's mistake. Let us seize the opportunity, take that second chance, and change.

---

11 Commentary to ibid.

Lech Lecha

Redefining Chessed

WE USUALLY DEFINE the word *chessed* as kindness, love, or compassion. And when we think of a *baal chessed*, what therefore comes to mind is a giver, a person dedicated to acts of loving-kindness. However, we will see, based on the profound thought of Rav Eliyahu Dessler, that this definition of *chessed* is not precise; it's too limiting. There are two *pesukim* in the Torah that prove this point:

- When the Torah prohibits a brother and sister from having intimacy, the Torah, remarkably, describes such an incestuous act as a "*chessed*."[1] That the Torah describes such a union as "*chessed*" is jarring. It is simply incongruous to translate *chessed* in this context as an act of kindness or compassion.

---

1   *Vayikra* 20:17.

- Likewise, in *Sefer Mishlei*, we are advised not to become involved in a quarrel, and, if we do become involved in one, to be careful not to betray any confidences, "lest he who hears revile you (*y'chasedcha*), and your infamy not be withdrawn."[2]

If *chessed*, at its root, means kindness or love, how can it serve to express condemnation and censure? This is not to say that the word *chessed* is not closely linked to kindness and giving. A *baal chessed* is certainly someone who is giving and loving. Rather, the above usages of the word *chessed* compel us to acknowledge that the word has a more basic meaning, and that acts of giving and loving-kindness are an expression of the *baal chessed*'s broader underlying personality. To explore and discover the root of the word *chessed* and the *chessed* personality, we must turn, of course, to the consummate *baal chessed*: Avraham Avinu.

In order to highlight Avraham's singularity, our sages often contrast him with two other well-known personalities: Iyov and Noach. For example, when Iyov complains to Hashem that since he has always been so generous to others, his suffering and privation are undeserved, Hashem responds by contrasting him with Avraham:

> Iyov, you have not even reached one half of the level of Avraham. You sit in your house and travelers enter. If one is used to eating meat, you give him meat; if one is used to drinking wine, you give him wine. Avraham does not act this way. He goes around the world looking for guests, and when he finds them, he brings them into his house. Even to one who is not used to eating meat he serves meat, and even to one who is not used to drinking wine, he serves wine. Moreover, he built a large house by the crossroads and laid out food and drink, and whoever wanted would enter, partake of the food, and bless G-d in Heaven. This is what gave Avraham pleasure. And whatever anybody asked for was available in Avraham's house.[3]

---

2 *Mishlei* 25:10.
3 *Avos deRabbi Nasan* 7:1.

As Rav Dessler explains, Iyov's generosity requires an external stimulus. Iyov acts out of a sense of pity and mercy. He doesn't actively seek the needy; only when his pity is aroused does Iyov give. And because Iyov requires exposure to the needy for inspiration, their habits frame and delimit his generosity; he provides them only with what they are used to. But while Iyov reacts, Avraham acts.[4]

Avraham is self-motivated. He acts independent of any external stimulus. Because he is internally driven to give and is not dependent on the presence of those in need, Avraham takes the initiative to seek out those who can benefit from his generosity. And since Avraham acts independently, free from outside influence, he is not circumscribed by his recipients' perceived needs and is able to offer them food they never imagined tasting.[5]

In the same vein, other sources indicate that Iyov is motivated to do acts of kindness because he wants to receive reward and avoid punishment.[6] Unlike Avraham who acts authentically, Iyov is driven by ulterior motives and external gain. To capture the difference between Iyov and Avraham concisely, we can say that while Iyov is a dependent, Avraham is an independent.

This essential difference between Avraham and Iyov, says Rav Dessler, is also the fundamental difference between Avraham and Noach. Unlike Noach who walks "with Hashem,"[7] Avraham walks "before Hashem."[8] Our sages, sensitive to this nuance, perceive Noach and Avraham at different stages of maturity:

> *Said Rabbi Yehudah: The matter may be compared to the case of a king who has two sons, one an adult, the other a child. He said to the child, "Walk with me," and to the adult, "Walk before me." So Avraham, who was strong, was told, "Walk before Me," while Noach, who was weak, "walked with G-d."*[9]

---

4   Eliyahu E. Dessler, *Strive for Truth: Volume III*, trans. Aryeh Carmell (Feldheim, 2004), p. 87.
5   Ibid.
6   For example, see BT *Sotah* 27b.
7   Bereishis 6:9.
8   Bereishis 17:1.
9   *Bereishis Rabbah* 30:10.

The *Maharal*, as quoted by Rav Dessler, explains that Noach's self-conscious awareness of Hashem's abiding presence animates him. Noach's righteousness and inspiration depend on the external stimulus of Hashem's presence. In contrast, Avraham, having internalized Hashem's values and ideals, no longer needs to feel close to and overtly conscious of Hashem's presence to be inspired and moved to do good. This distinction leads Rav Dessler to a shocking conclusion:

> *It seems that deveikus (clinging to Hashem) is not the highest achievement. What is beyond deveikus? The service of chessed! This is the pure service that flows from the depths of one's being, requiring no external or other type of aid whatsoever...The baal chessed does not require support; he has inner resources.*[10]

Noach who is a dependent, needing his feelings of closeness to Hashem to support and hold him up, is in this sense less mature and developed than Avraham, who is independent, resourceful, and self-sufficient. Because of these qualities, Avraham is the consummate *baal chessed*.[11]

If we define *chessed* more precisely as "independence," we can better appreciate the Torah's surprising use of the word, mentioned above:

- By labeling sibling incest as an act of *chessed*, the Torah conveys that such a union is an expression of independence. Turning internally within one's family of origin to cohabitate, and not needing to rely on external sources for a partner, is an act of independence. Because that kind of independence is perverse, though, it is forbidden.
- Similarly, *Mishlei* warns a slanderer that his unguarded speech will force him to become independent. As a result of his

---

[10] Eliyahu E. Dessler, *Strive for Truth (Volume III)*, trans. Aryeh Carmell (Feldheim, 2004), pp. 88–9.

[11] Ibid.

betrayal, he will be despised and condemned to isolation, where his enduring pariah status will compel him to rely exclusively on his own resources (*y'chasedcha*).

In the final analysis, the *baal chessed* is the source of his own loving-kindness. He is a pure "giver" because he takes nothing, not even external stimulus, inspiration, or motivation. The *baal chessed* has integrated Hashem's teachings so thoroughly that his righteousness and kindness flow instinctively from the very depths of his being. Indeed, says Rav Dessler, this is a very lofty level. But as the children of Avraham Avinu, we have been endowed with the DNA of a *baal chessed*. We are all predisposed with the potential to act independently — as *baalei chessed* in its fullest sense.

Vayeira

Glancing Back: Curiosity or Concern?

UNLIKE AVRAHAM AVINU, who serves his guests *ugos*, tasty cakes, Lot serves his guests *matzos*, plain, unflavored, and unleavened bread. Because the word *matzos* can be vocalized to be read as *matzus*, strife, the midrash sees an allusion to a conflict between Lot and his wife over the menu served to their guests. Lot asks his wife to give the strangers a little salt to flavor their meal. She refuses, concerned that doing so will "introduce in our town the ugly custom of having guests."[1]

What's challenging about this interaction is that Lot's wife only chastises him when he asks for salt on behalf of his guests. Why doesn't the original invitation to join him in their home disturb her? Wouldn't

---

1   *Bereishis Rabbah* 50:4.

hosting them in the first place introduce the vile custom of *hachnasas orchim* into Sodom?

Interestingly, salt appears explicitly in the text, later on in the episode. Although the angels warn Lot and his family not to look behind them as they flee, the Torah tells us that, "Lot's wife gazed behind him and she became a pillar of salt."[2] The *Radak* understands that her punishment is not unique. In fact, says the *Radak*, all the inhabitants of Sodom turn into either pillars of salt or pillars of sulphur.[3] As the *pasuk* in *Devarim* states, "Sulphur and salt, a conflagration of the entire land, like the upheaval of Sodom."[4] Similarly, the *Sefer HaGan*, an early commentary, edited and annotated by Rabbi Dr. Mitchell Orlian, interprets the *pasuk* to mean that because Lot's wife delays by looking back, she is consumed along with the rest of Sodom's citizens by the sulphur and salt storm that devours the city.[5]

Rashi, however, perceives a deeper meaning behind her transformation: Since Lot's wife sinned with salt, she is punished with salt.[6] For *Rashi*, Lot's wife is uniquely punished, measure for measure. The difficulty with *Rashi*'s interpretation, though, is that the "measure for measure" principle is not only stylistic, but substantive. If one is generous, he will be treated generously in return. If one is unforgiving, then in return, others will not be quick to pardon him. If one is careless with another's money, then he, in turn, will be robbed. Here, however, Lot's wife isn't mistreated as a traveler looking for hospitality in return for her own inhospitality. For withholding seasoning from her guests' food, her meal isn't served to her bland. Instead, because she is stingy with salt, she turns into a pillar of salt! How does the punishment fit the crime?

Whenever an extraordinary event takes place, there is a human tendency to treat the incident as a spectacle, a "sight to see," and not necessarily as something that demands a moral response. For example,

---

2   *Bereishis* 19:26.
3   Commentary to ibid.
4   *Devarim* 29:22.
5   Commentary to *Bereishis* 19:26.
6   Commentary to *Bereishis* 19:26.

instead of following the news, looking at pictures, and watching videos of a natural disaster out of consideration and concern for those affected, the tendency is to do so out of curiosity. Viewed as a novelty, a natural disaster, rather than eliciting feelings of compassion and empathy for the victims, is often experienced impersonally, as something merely to gawk at. And this tendency to respond with curiosity instead of concern doesn't only manifest during extremely unusual events, but even under milder conditions and for not so common occurrences, such as the arrival of exotic guests.

In Sodom, to respond to the unusual with curiosity instead of concern is not only a tendency, but a way of life. In Sodom, strangers are never treated with compassion and concern. At best, passersby are spectacles; at worst, easy victims. Consequently, Lot's wife has no qualms with Lot bringing home strangers. The exotic-looking fellows pique her interest and arouse her curiosity. In Sodom, providing guests plain, unflavored bread is acceptable, a necessary sacrifice to keep guests preoccupied and content long enough to satisfy the host's curiosity.

Lot, however, breaks with protocol when he asks for salt. Offering salt is an act of hospitality. Flavoring the meal is for the guest's benefit alone, without any self-serving outcome for the host. Providing salt would transform their guests from mere spectacles into subjects of concern. To do so, then, would be tantamount to introducing the detestable practice of *hachnasas orchim* into Sodom. Lot's wife therefore refuses. Later in the episode, when she stumbles and sins, measure for measure, Lot's wife turns into a pillar of salt — an unusual spectacle, an object of curiosity.

Lot, too, perceives his guests as a novelty, relating to them exclusively with curiosity and without concern. Because he experiences their visit in such a perverse, selfish way, Lot is prepared to sacrifice his own daughters to protect his own, momentary interests. For this reason — because of their shared proclivities — Lot and his wife are prohibited from looking upon the destruction of Sodom. The destruction is not meant as a spectacle to be curiously and impersonally gawked at. Only Avraham Avinu, who desperately pleads with Hashem to spare the people of Sodom, is allowed to gaze upon the destruction. Undoubtedly, Avraham would do so with a concerned and pained heart.

Responding to acts of G-d is part of the human experience. When disaster does strike, may we look at the devastation as the children of Avraham Avinu, who once gazed upon the destroyed plains of Sodom not with curiosity, but with compassion, care, and concern.

Chayei Sarah

Minchah's Contribution

AWAITING ELIEZER'S RETURN from Charan, Yitzchak Avinu goes out *"lasu'ach* in the field toward evening."[1] Based on a *pasuk* elsewhere,[2] where the phrase *"siach hasadeh"* means "trees of the field," the *Rashbam* interprets that Yitzchak heads out to the field to plant trees and to supervise production.[3] *Rashi*, however, interprets that Yitzchak goes out to the field to *daven*.[4] *Siach*, says *Rashi*, is an expression of *tefillah*, as in, "A prayer of one afflicted when he is faint and pours out his complaint (*sicho*) before Hashem."[5] *Rashi's* interpretation is informed by the Gemara, which learns

---

1   *Bereishis* 24:63.
2   *Bereishis* 2:5.
3   Commentary to *Bereishis* 24:63.
4   Ibid.
5   *Tehillim* 102:1.

from here that Yitzchak Avinu establishes the afternoon *tefillah* of *Minchah*.⁶

According to *Rashi*, why does the Torah present the source for *Minchah* so ambiguously, with a vague expression that could be interpreted entirely differently, as the *Rashbam*, in fact, does? Why doesn't the Torah use an unequivocal term to denote Yitzchak's *tefillah*?

Right before we read about Yitzchak heading into the field, the Torah records that he had recently returned from having gone to a place called Be'er Lechai Ro'i.⁷ Be'er Lechai Ro'i is the body of water where Hagar (in *parashas Lech Lecha*) encounters an angel, is told that Hashem has heard her afflictions, and is promised that her offspring will increase. Inspired by the revelation, Hagar names the place *Be'er Lechai Ro'i*, which means "the well of the living one appearing to me." Why does Yitzchak go there, of all places?

Rashi posits that Yitzchak didn't want his father to live alone as a widower. So he went to Be'er Lechai Ro'i to retrieve Hagar, who was presumably living there, to reunite her with Avraham.⁸

The *Seforno*, too, makes the connection between Be'er Lechai Ro'i and Hagar, but explains the circumstances very differently. According to the *Seforno*, Yitzchak goes to Be'er Lechai Ro'i to daven in the very place where Hagar's prayers were once answered.⁹ What, though, is so special about that occurrence? His mother's and father's *tefillos* were also answered, time and time again. Why does Yitzchak need to draw inspiration from Hagar and Be'er Lechai Ro'i?

The *Seforno* gives us the key to unlock this puzzle in his commentary on *parashas Lech Lecha*.¹⁰ There, he elucidates why, after her divine encounter, Hagar calls Hashem the "G-d of Vision (*Ro'i*),"¹¹ and thus the name of the well, *Be'er Lechai Ro'i*. Hagar, says the *Seforno*, realizes

---

6   BT *Berachos* 26b.
7   *Bereishis* 24:62.
8   Commentary to ibid.
9   Ibid.
10 *Bereishis* 16:13.
11 Ibid.

for the first time that Hashem's sight and purview know no bounds: Hashem's scope of concern and influence is not limited to the confines of Avraham's house, but encompasses all places.

Perhaps, this is why Yitzchak, not yet knowing whether or not Eliezer has succeeded, goes to Be'er Lechai Ro'i for inspiration. Conscious of the fact that Eliezer's mission takes him far away from Avraham's house, Yitzchak davens for his success in the very place where Hashem's limitless vision was once clearly demonstrated.

It is no coincidence, therefore, that the Torah juxtaposes Yizchak's journey to Be'er Lechai Ro'i to his establishment of *Minchah*. Yitzchak doesn't just add another *tefillah*; he introduces a new dimension of *tefillah*. Unlike *Shacharis*, which is done in a set and fixed place, close to home, *Minchah* is often experienced outside one's community, in the midst of the workday, and wherever one finds himself. The salient feature of *Minchah* is that no matter where we are throughout the day, we are assured that we remain visible to Hashem and under His sphere of concern. During *Minchah*, we daven to Hashem, the "G-d of Vision."

Personally speaking, one of my most meaningful and spiritual *tefillos* has been a *Minchah*. I was driving on the interstate back from Philadelphia, where I had been *menachem avel* a friend of mine who lost his father. At some point along the way, I realized I might not make it back in time for *Minchah*. So I pulled over into one of the large Food and Rest areas along the highway. Inside, I found a semi-isolated spot in between some vending machines. There, I carved out of a piece of Pennsylvania my own, private space to stand before Hashem. It was an exhilarating experience to feel, in the middle of nowhere, still in the presence of Hashem. That *Minchah* was like no other, and certainly like no *Shacharis* or *Maariv* I ever davened. During that *Minchah*, I experienced Hashem, the G-d of Vision.

Perhaps this added dimension explains why the Torah presents *Minchah* couched in terms that can just as well mean agricultural activity, instead of using a conventional phrase for *tefillah*. The Torah is not being intentionally misleading; rather, the Torah is conveying the unique quality of Yitzchak's *tefillah*, how it is different than his father's

Shacharis. Yitzchak davens to Hashem, not in a fixed spot in the house of his father, but out in the world, even as he cultivates and supervises his various commercial activities. When Yitzchak goes out into the field to work, he is able to carve out his own, private space to daven to Hashem. To Hashem, the G-d of Vision.

Toldos

The US Constitution, Megillas Esther, and Eisav

ONE OF THE most bewildering parts of the Torah is the passage that details Yitzchak Avinu's wish to bless and, by doing so, pass on the Abrahamic legacy to Eisav instead of to Yaakov Avinu, the more obvious candidate. How does Yitzchak get it so wrong? What is it about Eisav that so enamors him?

Perhaps, the question should be put differently: What is it about Yaakov that displeases Yitzchak?

There is an ongoing culture war in the United States of America between the religious right and the secular left. What is at stake is no less than the character and identity of the country. The religious right defends its position by arguing that the country was founded by Christians and with Christian values and beliefs. The counterargument of the secular left is twofold:

1. It doesn't matter, they argue, what the country's origins and traditions are, because modern, liberal-minded man isn't held hostage to the past, especially when it is fraught with backwardness, arbitrariness, inequality, oppression, etc.
2. America, the left asserts, has *not* always been a Christian country. Rather, America is a religiously neutral country, founded on secular enlightenment principles of inalienable rights and freedoms, including the right and freedom to reject not only Christianity but all forms of religious belief. After all, they gleefully note, the United States Constitution (the country's foundational document) makes not one reference to G-d.

The conspicuous absence of G-d's name in the Constitution was not lost on its framers. During the constitutional convention and ratification, heated debates erupted over the glaring omission. How, many wondered, can a nation come into being without acknowledging its belief in G-d? Others, the forerunners of modern-day liberals, argued that prudence informed the carefully chosen words of the document. In the spirit of tolerance, the Constitution was rendered religiously neutral. There were even some who defended the omission from both a humanistic and religious perspective. To attach the Name of G-d to the document, they argued, would be an abuse of G-d's Name and a manipulation of the people. The administrative quality and efficacy of the Constitution should speak for itself without needing sanction from a higher power. As one writer in *American Mercury* (February 18, 1788), by the name of Elihu, asserted:

> *The most shining part, the most brilliant circumstance in honor of the framers of the Constitution is their avoiding all appearance of craft, declining to dazzle even the superstitious by a hint of grace or ghostly knowledge. They come to us in the plain language of common sense and propose to our understanding a system of government as the invention of mere human wisdom;*

no deity comes down to dictate it, not even a G-d appears in a dream to propose any part of it.[1]

In this view, throughout history, throngs of people have been tricked by those who presumed to speak in G-d's Name into adopting various systems of beliefs and politics. Invoking G-d's Name in the Constitution would echo this insidious practice and preclude the masses from examining the document critically and on its own merits.

What this last opinion underscores is that using and speaking in G-d's Name is not always just. Even G-d's Name is not immune from exploitation and abuse. We are warned: "Do not take the Name of Hashem your G-d in vain"[2] not only to protect against familiarity and irreverence, but to ensure that we don't misuse Hashem's Name for our own purposes, whether to manipulate others or to deceive ourselves.

Hashem, as we know, is invisible. It's His distinguishing feature. Still, His invisibility, as philosophers, psychologists, and anthropologists from Hume to Freud to Becker have noted, is a source of acute anxiety. It's quite a challenge for human beings to find solace and security in an abstract being. We should not underestimate the psychological benefits of being able to hug, kiss, bow, and give gifts to a tangible G-d. Just think of how good we feel when we walk into a doctor's office, of the comfort and security we derive by his mere presence and aura of expertise. For this reason, idolatry was so appealing to Jews throughout Biblical times: it gave Jews the opportunity to represent Hashem in a concrete and visible way.

The next best thing to representing Hashem visually is to do so audibly. By invoking Hashem's Name, we manifest His presence. Almost as much as an idol can assuage a person's anxieties and insecurities, so can the articulation of His Name. It's no coincidence that the prohibition against idolatry and taking Hashem's Name in vain, together, comprise their

---

1   Quoted in Jon Meacham, *American Gospel: G-d, the Founding Fathers, and the Making of a Nation* (Random House, 2006), pp. 97–8.
2   *Shemos* 20:7.

own independent section in the Torah.[3] And attaching Hashem's Name to our opinions and endeavors can be a way to draw not only comfort and security, but, as we have seen, validation. By invoking Hashem's Name, we can free ourselves from the need to justify our views and actions. If Hashem's Name is associated with it, it must be right and good and true.

What emerges is that frequent usage of Hashem's Name may indicate overdependency and moral weakness. Ironically, then, the omission of Hashem's Name may be a sign not of secularism but religious maturity. This phenomenon and the confusion it can create is, perhaps, the basis for Yitzchak's error.

Despite Yitzchak's intentions, Yaakov, as we know, takes matters into his own hands to attain the *berachos*. During the ruse, however, Yaakov almost makes a fatal mistake — he mentions the Name of Hashem. Asked by Yitzchak how he so quickly found and prepared the game, Yaakov responds, "Because Hashem, your G-d, caused it to happen for me."[4] Not used to hearing Eisav utter the Name of Hashem, Yitzchak demands that Yaakov approach so he may feel his skin.

The *Ramban* struggles to follow Yitzchak's logic. Presumably, Yitzchak does not perceive Eisav as a nonbeliever; after all, Yitzchak is willing and eager to bestow his blessings upon him. Why, then, is Yitzchak's suspicion aroused when Yaakov, dissembling as Eisav, pronounces Hashem's Name? And, if indeed, it was not Eisav's habit, at all, to mention the Name of Hashem in conversation, why would Yitzchak favor him over Yaakov? The Ramban answers:

> *Perhaps Yitzchak thought to himself that because Eisav was a man of the field (Bereishis 25:27), and his mind was concentrated on hunting, he refrained from mentioning the Name of Heaven out of fear lest he mention it in an unclean place or without the proper intention. And in his father's eyes this was considered an indication of Eisav's fear of Heaven.[5]*

---

3   *Shemos* 20:2–7.
4   *Bereishis* 27:20.
5   Commentary to ibid.

Based on our discussion, however, the *Ramban* doesn't need to go so far. Yitzchak intends to bless Eisav because he sees his reticence as a sign of righteousness. Eisav, Yitzchak erroneously thinks, has internalized and integrated his awareness of Hashem so thoroughly into his psyche that he needs neither visual nor audio aids in order to engage the world and repair it. Because of the way Eisav comports himself, he is mistaken for a religiously mature, independent, and courageous individual. Eisav, it seems, has the qualities needed to implement Hashem's vision for the world. Yaakov, on the other hand — the "pious man who remained in the tents,"[6] — comes across as relatively underdeveloped. He reminds Yitzchak of Noach, another pious individual who lived in isolation, first in a cave, then in an ark.

Yitzchak, of course, is incorrect. About both of them:

- Eisav omits Hashem's Name from his lexicon because he neglects Hashem, because he is wicked. Indeed, not using Hashem's Name can be misleading, especially if you take it for granted that your son is fundamentally good.
- Yitzchak also errs in that he underestimates Yaakov. It isn't until Yaakov's ruse that Yitzchak (and the reader) sees Yaakov's potential. It is then, when he dons not only Eisav's clothes, but Eisav's identity as a "hunter, a man of the field"[7] that Yaakov demonstrates that he is capable of assuming the mantle of leadership and the responsibility to engage the world and transform it in the image of the Torah.

We live in complicated days:

- On the one hand, G-d's Great Name is abused on a daily basis. Lies, atrocities, and terrorism are all perpetrated in His Name.
- On the other hand, secularism and atheism are on the rise.

Each of these camps feed off the ever-growing extremism of the other. We find ourselves in the midst of a vicious cycle. What are we to

---

6   *Bereishis* 25:27.
7   Ibid.

do? Do we consciously refrain from using Hashem's Name in order to demonstrate that authentic religious living need not rely on (and misuse) G-d's Name? Or, must we invoke and call out in Hashem's Name whenever we can in order to show that our wholesome and meaningful lifestyles are an expression of godliness?

When Boaz, in *Megillas Rus*, perceives that the Name of Hashem is becoming obsolete, he institutes the practice of greeting one another with it. Our sages observe that Boaz is well aware this practice is in direct violation of "Do not take the Name of Hashem your G-d in vain." Nevertheless, his policy is a necessary evil; Boaz feels compelled to do so "in order to preserve Hashem's Torah."[8] Mordechai and Esther, in contrast, compose a book that omits Hashem's Name. Writing in a pagan society, they are acutely aware that Hashem's Name is vulnerable to abuse, by Jew and non-Jew alike.

In our time, when the Name of G-d is simultaneously being abused by believers and derided by nonbelievers, what are we to do? How are we to end this vicious cycle that is tearing our world apart? Do we act like Boaz or like Mordechai?

---

8   BT *Berachos* 54a. See *Rashi*'s commentary ibid.

Vayeitzei

Who's Carrying Who?

AFTER YAAKOV AVINU awakens from his dream, he sets out to continue on his journey to Charan. The Torah describes Yaakov's departure as follows: "Yaakov lifted his feet and went toward the land of the easterners."[1] Why does the Torah choose this unusual expression, "lifted his feet"? What is meant to be conveyed? Our sages, sensitive to the text, are troubled by this and offer a couple of explanations:

- The expression is an idiom that captures a reluctance to leave one's current place. An individual who "lifts his feet" is, so to speak, compelling himself to depart despite his wishes to stay. Having experienced a divine revelation at this rest stop, Yaakov longed to stay at this holy site.[2]

---

1   *Bereishis* 29:1.
2   Cited in, Menachem M. Kasher, *Torah Shelemah: Volume IV* (Torah Shelemah Institute, 1992), p. 1153.

- The expression is an idiom that connotes light-footedness. After being blessed by Hashem, Yaakov had a spring in his step as he set out to Charan.[3]

In addition to these two interpretations, perhaps we can suggest another meaning, one that, as Yaakov sets out to face Lavan, communicates Yaakov's ability not only to withstand adverse influences, but to impact his surroundings positively.

As we know, the Torah prohibits thirty-nine *melachos* on Shabbos. Since Hashem refrained from creativity on the seventh day of the week, we abstain as well. The creative aspects of all the *melachos* are self-evident. Except for one.

Hotza'ah, the act of carrying an object from a private domain to a public domain, and vice versa, is considered a *melachah*, and it is prohibited on Shabbos. The reason for this classification is unclear; no transformation takes place when an object is moved from one place to another. So where is the creativity in transferring an object? The classic commentators on the Gemara are vexed by this difficulty and as a result, deem *hotza'ah* as an "incomplete" or "inferior" *melachah*.[4] Still, to whatever degree, *hotza'ah* is considered a creative act by the Torah. Why?

The implication of the prohibition of *hotza'ah* is that objects have both intrinsic and extrinsic characteristics. Not only is an object defined by its inherent shape, size, color, material, and functionality, but by its location. By way of illustration, the very same object found in a lecture hall, synagogue, and *beis midrash* is called, respectively, a lectern, a pulpit, and a *shtender*. Its location determines how it is described.

This idea is reflected in the laws of *hashavas aveidah*, returning lost objects. If a lost object that is found has a *siman* (an identifying mark) on it, the finder cannot keep the item. Instead, he is obligated to announce his find, in the hope that the owner will identify and retrieve his object by providing the *siman* — identification. Why is one only

---

3   Ibid. See also *Rashi* in his commentary to *Bereishis* 29:1.
4   For example, see *Tosafos*, BT *Shabbos* 2a, s.v. *Pashat*.

obligated to announce an object that has a *siman*? At first glance, the answer is obvious: only if the item has a distinct mark would the finder ever be able to verify who the true owner is. While this is true, there is much evidence in the laws of *hashavas aveidah* that there is another dimension to the factor of *siman*: only a lost item that is personalized, that is indispensable in its owner's eyes, needs to be returned. If an item has no distinct mark, if it resembles every other item of its kind, then the item is replaceable and need not be returned.

Concerning valid *simanim*, our sages dispute whether or not location can serve as a *siman*.[5] One issue at the basis of their argument is whether the ability to provide information as to *where* the item was lost is conclusive enough evidence of ownership. Another underlying issue at the heart of their argument is whether an object, without any distinction other than its location, is considered unique. The position that a lost object can be identified by its location is of the view that an object is defined not only by its intrinsic characteristics, but by its extrinsic characteristics as well. An item in one location is different than an item of the very same make in another location. So if an owner of a lost object knows its location, then the item is considered to be personalized and must be returned.

Hotza'ah, therefore, is forbidden on Shabbos for its transformative effect, albeit a small one. By moving an item from a private domain to a public domain, or vice versa, the transporter has created something different. He has redefined the item by giving it a new location, an updated extrinsic characteristic.

If this approach is correct, though, *hotza'ah* would be limited only to objects that are indeed redefined by their location. Any entity whose identity is *not* significantly shaped by location would not be subject to *hotza'ah* and could be transported on Shabbos. Indeed, this is exactly what we find. When it comes to *hotza'ah*, our sages disagree whether or not one is allowed to transport an animal on Shabbos.[6] Those who permit doing so base their view on the principle: *chai nosei es atzmo*,

---

5   BT *Bava Metzia* 22b.
6   BT *Shabbos* 97a.

that a living thing carries itself. Even when lifted and carried, a living creature will, to some degree, bear its own weight.

Interestingly, while the sages argue about carrying animals, everyone agrees that it is permissible to transport a human being. It is axiomatic that a person "carries himself." In other words, a human being is not subject to the prohibition of *hotza'ah* because carrying a person is not a creative act. Since a human being is not automatically influenced and shaped by his surroundings, he is not comparable to a passive object and is not defined by his location. Instead, a human being transcends his location. A human being carries himself.

So far, we have come across entities that are carried by others and entities that carry themselves:

- Objects that are carried by others are defined by their location.
- Human beings who carry themselves are not necessarily affected by their location.

But there is one more category of existence that still needs to be discussed.

Concerning the *Aron*, the Ark of Hashem that houses the *Luchos*, the Torah warns us never to remove its poles. Even when stationary, in no need to be carried, the *Aron* is to remain with its poles.[7] This law underscores that the *Aron*'s poles are not in place to enable transportation because, fundamentally, the *Aron* doesn't need poles to be lifted and transported. It is self-sufficient. In fact, the opposite is true: The *Aron* is *nosei es nosav*, it carries those who carry it.[8]

Based on our analysis, this means that the *Aron* is uniquely different from other entities. While other objects are defined by their location, and human beings transcend their location, the *Aron* *influences* its location: it devastates enemy armies[9] and splits rivers.[10] Because the *Aron*

---

7   BT *Yoma* 72a, based on *Shemos* 25:15.
8   BT *Sotah* 35a.
9   *Bamidbar* 10:35.
10 *Yehoshua* 3:15–17.

symbolizes the Torah, its unique feature reflects what the Torah can and sets out to do: to impact, to shape, and to transform culture.

The ability to carry those who carry it is not limited to the *Aron* but to anything that embodies the Torah. "Yaakov lifted his feet and went toward the land of the easterners." Yaakov Avinu, too, carries that which carries him. Not only can he transcend his environment, Yaakov impacts it. As *Rashi* explains the opening *pasuk* of *parashas Vayeitzei* (that seems to superfluously relate that Yaakov departs from Be'er Sheva):

> *The extra phrase tells us that the departure of a tzaddik from a place makes an impression, for at the time that a tzaddik is in a city, he is its magnificence, he is its splendor, he is its grandeur. Once he has departed from there, its magnificence has gone away, its splendor has gone away, its grandeur has gone away.*[11]

Along the journey from his father's household in search of a wife, Hashem appears to Yaakov and promises him success. Yaakov will not be adversely affected by his new surroundings; instead, he will be a source of blessing.[12] When Yaakov sets out on the final phase of his journey to the house of the unscrupulous Lavan, the Torah shares with us the source of Hashem's confidence in Yaakov: he carries that which carries him.

---

11   Commentary to *Bereishis* 28:10.
12   See *Bereishis* 28:14, 29:10, and 30:27.

Influential Images

AFTER EXTENSIVE RESEARCH and having interviewed an array of historians, curators, and photographers over a three-year period, *Time* magazine published a list of the one hundred most influential photographs ever taken. A list comprised not of the most famous pictures, per se, nor of the ones taken by the most renowned photographers. Rather, it was a list of the images that have had the most impact on the most people. For example, the list includes the 1943 Jewish Boy Surrendering in Warsaw, the 1968 Black Power Salute, and the 1989 Tank Man in Tiananmen Square.

The list is thought-provoking: Which images portrayed in the Torah have had the most far-reaching and lasting effect? When considering some images in the Torah, what immediately came to mind is the image of Yaakov Avinu's ladder, firmly rooted on the ground but whose head reached the heavens, with rising and descending angels upon it, and Hashem hovering above. Still, was this vision and image influential? In other words, the *Time* magazine list may force us to reexamine and rethink the dream. Why is Yaakov shown this vision now? Why is it necessary? Or, put another way, what would the course of history have been like had Yaakov *not* seen this image or experienced the dream? In order to answer these questions, we need to try and get into Yaakov's mind before the dream and see what preoccupies his thoughts as he flees Beer Sheva and heads to Charan.

There is a discrepancy in the *pesukim* about the stones Yaakov takes to rest his head upon:

- At first, the Torah says that "Yaakov took from the stones of

that place,"¹ which implies that he gathered a bunch of stones.
- Yet the next morning, when Yaakov wakes up, the Torah speaks only of a singular stone: "Yaakov...took the stone that he had put under his head, set it up as a pillar, and poured oil on top of it."²

To reconcile the *pesukim*, our sages suggest that the many stones Yaakov originally takes merge overnight into one. The sages argue about how many stones Yaakov initially takes and the meaning behind the merger:

> *Rabbi Yehudah said: He took twelve stones and said, "Avraham didn't establish twelve tribes. Yitzchak didn't establish twelve tribes. If these twelve stones merge with each other, then I'll know that I am destined to establish the twelve tribes."*
>
> *Rabbi Nechemiah said: He took three stones and said, "Hashem conferred His Name upon Avraham. Hashem conferred His Name upon Yitzchak. If these three stones merge together, then I'll know that Hashem will designate His Name upon me."*
>
> *The Rabbis said: He took two stones and said, "Avraham begot unsuitable children, Yishmael and the sons of Keturah. And Yitzchak begot unsuitable descendents, Eisav and his chieftains. As for me, if these two stones merge, I'll know that none of my children will be unsuitable.³*

There is a common thread running through all three positions: Yaakov Avinu, when he goes to sleep, is plagued with self-doubt. Yaakov is uncertain if he is worthy enough to produce the twelve tribes, to be one of the Avos, or to produce only righteous children.

What is the source of his self-doubt?

The *Abarbanel* posits that Yaakov is tormented by the possibility that his scheme to take the *berachos* from Eisav was deemed unethical in the

---

1 Bereishis 28:11.
2 Bereishis 28:18.
3 Bereishis Rabbah 68:11.

eyes of Hashem. As a result, he fears he will live an accursed life. This is why the vision is shown to Yaakov now. The image of the ladder and angels, accompanied by Divine promises and blessings, demonstrates unambiguously to Yaakov that what he had done concerning Eisav was right in Hashem's eyes, and that he is deserving and worthy to become the patriarch with the distinction of bearing the twelve tribes.[4]

It is a truism that conviction begets confidence, which in turn begets courage. The inverse, of course, is also true. Yaakov, who lacks conviction (and confidence) as he flees his father's household, needs the Divine vision to withstand and survive Lavan. Without it, the course of history, it seems, would have been drastically different. Confusion and lack of confidence would not have served Yaakov well in the home of the conniving and scheming Lavan. Instead, with the image of the ladder, angels, and Hashem seared in his mind, Yaakov is armed with the conviction, confidence, and courage to outwit Lavan.

From time to time, when faced with challenges, adversity, or doubt, we can all utilize images from our tradition, our family history, and our personal past to strengthen our resolve and confidence. At times, we may even have to create our own mental images of what can and ought to be in order to inspire and propel us to achieve them. Looking back, after a lifetime of achievement, we might, one day, put together our own personal list of the top images that left a lasting impression on us.

---

[4] Commentary to *Bereishis* 28:12–15.

Vayishlach

The Anonymous Hero

PEGGY NOONAN, COLUMNIST for *The Wall Street Journal*, is a best-selling author of seven books on American politics, history, and culture. Her memoir, *What I Saw at the Revolution: A Political Life in the Reagan Era*, chronicles her years as a primary speechwriter and special assistant to President Reagan. In the chapter entitled "Challenger," she recalls the tragic explosion of the space shuttle Challenger and the speech she wrote for the president, eulogizing the seven astronauts. At one point in the chapter, Noonan reflects on the art of writing a standard eulogy, one given under more typical circumstances:

> *I love eulogies. They are the most moving kind of speech because they attempt to pluck meaning from the fog...It is a challenge to look at life and organize our thoughts about it and try to*

explain to ourselves what it meant, and the most moving part is the element of implicit celebration.

Most people aren't appreciated enough, and the bravest things we do in our lives are usually known only to ourselves. No one throws ticker tape on the man who chose to be faithful to his wife, on the lawyer who didn't take drug money, or the daughter who held her tongue again and again. All this anonymous heroism. A eulogy gives us the chance to celebrate it.[1]

Noonan's turn of phrase, "anonymous heroism," can help us better understand a difficulty in this *parashah*.

In *Sefer Shoftim* we are told that Devorah, the prophetess, judge, and leader of the Jewish people, would customarily sit "under the tree of Devorah."[2] *Rashi* interprets that this tree was owned by Devorah herself; she was a wealthy person, who owned much land, and she would sit and meet with members of the Jewish community on her property, under her very own tree.[3]

The *Abarbanel*, however, suggests that the "tree of Devorah" was not the tree of the famous leader Devorah, but the tree of a different, lesser-known Devorah.

After Yaakov Avinu's battle with the angel, his encounter with Eisav, and the conflict at Shechem, the Torah records that, "Devorah, the wet-nurse of Rivkah, died, and she was buried below Beis El, under the tree; and he named it *Alon Bachus* — the weeping tree."[4] According to the *Abarbanel*, Devorah the prophetess would sit under this very tree, under the weeping tree, which the other Devorah (Rivkah Imeinu's wet-nurse) was buried.[5] The question, of course, begs itself: Why does Devorah the prophetess sit specifically under the tree of Devorah the wet-nurse?

---

1 Peggy Noonan, *What I Saw at the Revolution: A Political Life in the Reagan Era* (Random House, 2006), p. 253.
2 *Shoftim* 4:5.
3 Commentary to ibid.
4 *Bereishis* 35:8.
5 Commentary to *Shoftim* 4:5.

Moreover, why are we even told about Devorah the wet-nurse, a seemingly insignificant figure? Why mention her death and burial at all?

In the twelfth century, Northwest Africa and Spain were invaded by the Muslim sect, the Almoheds, who promoted a policy of forced conversion to Islam. As a result, many Jews were compelled to either publicly affirm their belief in the Muslim prophet or die a martyr's death. One such Jew, who opted not to give up his life, inquired of a rabbi whether he would gain any merit by secretly fulfilling and observing as many mitzvos as he could. The rabbi replied that the performance of any mitzvah by someone who has made a profession of faith to Islam was not only meaningless, but sinful.

The *Rambam*, in his *Iggeres HaShmad* (Letter on Martyrdom) adamantly rejects the rabbi's all-or-nothing attitude. He makes his case on two bases:

- First, he affirms the significance and value of a single mitzvah performed under any and all conditions.
- Second, he expands the range and definition of heroism by stressing that acts of *kiddush Hashem* are not confined to acts of martyrdom. As the *Rambam* states:

> *When a person fulfills one of the commandments, and no other motive impels him save the love of G-d and His service, he has publicly sanctified G-d's Name. So also, if he enjoys a good reputation he has sanctified G-d's Name. They say about such a person: "See how lovely are the ways of so-and-so who is learned in Torah, how proper his deeds."*

For the *Rambam*, great feats are not limited to dramatic moments, when everything is on the line. Instead, religious and moral heroism can be achieved in everyday life by leading a Torah lifestyle. Anonymous heroism, such as routine commitment, daily loyalty, ordinary sacrifices, and everyday acts of restraint, are all acts of *kiddush Hashem*.

The Torah's treatment of the death and burial of Devorah the wet-nurse reflects the *Rambam*'s sentiment. After we read about Yaakov's epic victory over the angel, his courageous encounter with Eisav, and Shimon and Levi's daring rescue of their abducted sister Dinah, the Torah turns its attention to Devorah the wet-nurse. By recording her death and burial, the Torah demonstrates that Judaism does not exclusively admire sensational heroic acts performed in the face of extraordinary circumstances.

Just as much, Judaism idealizes the anonymous hero who consistently and reliably impacts the lives of others. So, in the wake of dramatic heroic acts achieved by famous personalities, Yaakov and his family mourn the loss of their anonymous hero, Devorah the family wet-nurse, who was loving and devoted and faithful.

The Torah's insistence on expanding the scope of heroism was not lost on Yaakov's illustrious descendant many centuries later. Devorah, the prophetess, judge, and leader was a national hero, who, in that role, certainly sanctified G-d's Name. She was also a mother, a wife, a daughter, a sister, a friend, a neighbor. So Devorah the prophetess would sit under the tree of Devorah the wet-nurse to remind herself that Judaism is also about the everyday, private, heroic acts. Wanting to be an anonymous hero even more than a public one, Devorah sits under that tree for inspiration.

Likewise, we all have that "tree" we can go to and sit under. We all have that individual, or individuals, whether they are still with us or not, who have been our anonymous heroes. And when we sit under their tree, we recall their loyalty and integrity, their abiding love, and, especially, their everyday sacrifices on our behalf. May their shade inspire us to become anonymous heroes for others.

Vayeishev

Glue Is More Righteous than Velcro

IN 1960, NEARLY seventy percent of American adults were married; fifty years later, only about half are. As a result, eight times as many children are born out of wedlock.

Back then, sixty-six percent of twenty-somethings were married; today, just twenty-six percent are. Cohabitation, whereby couples live together — and sometimes have children together — but do not legally formalize their relationship, has become a popular alternative to marriage. In 1970, there were five hundred thousand cohabitating couples in the United States of America; currently, there are over five million.

Although more serious and longer lasting than other types of relationships, relative to marriage, cohabitation is more casual and transient, characterized by a smaller degree of commitment. There are fewer strings attached. While commitment and permanence are the hallmarks of marriage, convenience often informs the choice of cohabitation. As

Seth Eisenberg, president and CEO of the PAIRS Foundation, one of the biggest relationship-education operations in the country, puts it: "Marriage is like glue. You can build something with it. Living together is like Velcro."[1] The qualitative difference between families organized by glue instead of Velcro is a lesson learned the hard way in this *parashah*.

After Yosef is abducted, sold, and taken down to Egypt, the Torah briefly turns its attention to Yehudah: "It was at that time that Yehudah went down from his brothers and turned away toward an Adullamite man whose name was Chirah."[2] Commenting on the *pasuk*, the midrash says:

> **It was at that time:** *The Shevatim were involved with the sale of Yosef. Yosef was involved with sackcloth and fasting. Yaakov was involved with sackcloth and fasting. Yehudah was involved with finding a wife. Hakadosh Baruch Hu was involved with creating the light of Melech HaMashiach.*[3]

The midrash highlights that, although from our perspective things at the time looked bleak for Yaakov's family and for the future of Am Yisrael, at the very same time the seeds of our ultimate redemption were being sown by the Master of the Universe. Still, while the midrash's main point is incontrovertible, its presentation of the events is problematic. What does the midrash mean that, at the time the *Shevatim* were preoccupied with the sale of Yosef, Yosef was grieving and Yaakov was disconsolate and Yehudah was courting? These events all happened *after* the sale of Yosef, not during! Perhaps a closer look at Yehudah's story will shed some light on this obscure midrash.

After Yehudah marries, he has three sons, Er, Onan, and Sheilah. Er, we are told, marries the beautiful Tamar, only to be struck down by Hashem for avoiding having children with her. The *Bechor Shor* explains that Er avoids having children because raising them would

---

1 Belinda Luscombe, "Marriage, What's It Good For?" *Time* magazine, Nov. 2010.
2 *Bereishis* 38:1.
3 *Bereishis Rabbah* 81:1.

be too inconvenient and infringe on his lifestyle.⁴ Onan, after having been asked by Yehudah to perform *yibum* to perpetuate his dead brother's legacy, is also struck down by Hashem for failing in his familial duty to have a child with Tamar. The Torah informs us that Onan wasn't interested in assuming the responsibility of rearing a child that would legally be considered Er's, not his.⁵ Both Er and Onan make their choices based on self-interests and convenience, not on values of commitment, loyalty, and sacrifice. For the two of them, family is Velcro, not glue.

When Yehudah refuses to give his last surviving son, Sheilah, to Tamar, she rightfully schemes to have Yehudah father a child with her. When it is discovered that she (still legally bound to Sheilah) is pregnant by another man, Yehudah condemns her to death. Not wanting to humiliate him, Tamar exclaims that the owner of the objects in her possession (taken as collateral for her services) is the father of her child. Yehudah, suddenly realizing that she was the woman he was intimate with, publically declares, "*Tzadkah mimeni*," which, in its plain meaning is rendered: "She is more righteous than me."⁶ *Rashi*, though, interprets Yehudah's words as a clipped expression: *Tzadkah* — She is right in her words; *mimeni* — it is from me that she is pregnant."⁷

Inspired by this reading, perhaps we can suggest a different interpretation of Yehudah's expression. In order to do so, we must first properly understand the midrash we began with.

When the midrash says that, "At the time the *Shevatim* were preoccupied with the sale of Yosef, Yosef was grieving and Yaakov was disconsolate and Yehudah was courting," it doesn't mean at the time the brothers were engaged with the logistics of the sale. Rather, the midrash means that at the time the brothers were preoccupied with the consequences of having sold Yosef, Yosef was grieving and Yaakov was disconsolate and Yehudah was courting. While the brothers were

---

4   Commentary to *Bereishis* 38:7.
5   As explained by *Bechor Shor* in his commentary to *Bereishis* 38:9.
6   *Bereishis* 38:26.
7   Commentary to ibid.

struggling with the fact they had caused their beloved father so much pain and suffering, Yehudah was *dating*.

Yehudah, explains the *Bechor Shor*, unable to confront his father's anguish, leaves home.[8] As a result of Yosef's abduction, life in his father's home had become too challenging for him, and it was no longer convenient to remain by his father's side. So, like Velcro, Yehudah detaches himself from his father's household to build afresh his own household, away from his father's pain.

Later, when confronted with the evidence of his disloyalty to Tamar, he courageously admits, "*Tzadkah mimeni*."

- *Tzadkah* — She is right in her words;
- *Mimeni* — This whole tragic episode is because of me. My boys learned *from me*. Er and Onan saw the way I valued family life, the way I viewed family as Velcro and not as glue. They simply followed in my footsteps.

It is only now that Yehudah finally realizes the error of his ways: for leaving his father when he needed him the most, and for having sold Yosef in the first place — for ripping the family apart.

It is a human tendency to gravitate toward ideologies, institutions, and lifestyles that satisfy our base desires. Cohabitation is a framework that is appealing precisely because it satisfies one's wants at a seemingly small cost. What is not readily apparent to its adherents, however, is the hidden cost that comes with a family organized by Velcro. In the long run, the instability and insecurity that it breeds, along with the ethic of selfishness and instant gratification that it promotes, harm all those that are involved.

The Torah, with its broad outlook, provides us with instruction on how to arrange our family lives in a way that maximizes our well-being. The institution of marriage is founded on glue: a relationship based on commitment and permanence. In marriage, families are nurtured on an ethic of giving, responsibility, and hard work, all within a framework

---

8   Commentary to *Bereishis* 38:1.

that provides the stability and security generally necessary to successfully pass on values and to nurture healthy and wholesome individuals.

This is the lesson Yehudah and his family learn: glue is more effective than Velcro. Marriage is more righteous — and stronger — than cohabitation.

Mikeitz

A Silent Prayer

IT IS STRIKING. Throughout Yosef's ordeal, from the moment he is snatched by his jealous brothers to the moment he is brought before Pharaoh with his future still very much in the balance, Yosef never davens. Not once. The Torah records not one "Please, Hashem, save me." No "Please, Hashem, bring me back to my father." Not even a "Please, Hashem, help me impress Pharaoh." Avraham Avinu davens on behalf of Sodom, Yitzchak Avinu desperately davens for children, and Yaakov Avinu davens to return home safely and successfully. But from Yosef: silence. And if we must insist that Yosef indeed davened, why doesn't the Torah share his pleas and petitions the way it does by his father, grandfather, and great-grandfather?

Perhaps, through the trials and tribulations of Yosef, the Torah presents us with a different framework for thinking about *tefillah*.

The conventional understanding of *tefillah*, which was made popular by the *Ramban*, sees *tefillah* as an outpouring of the heart. The supplicant is involved in communicating his needs and his desires to Hashem, in hope that Hashem will grant them. For the *Ramban*, *tefillah* is theologically meaningful because it is presupposes Hashem's kindness toward us and His willingness to listen and respond.

The *Rambam*, however, has a completely different conception of what *tefillah* is. He characterizes *tefillah* as a form of worship. According to him, when the Torah enjoins us, "Worship Hashem"[1] and "Serve Him with all your heart,"[2] it refers to *tefillah*. For the *Rambam*, *tefillah* is uniquely a "worship of the heart."[3] This reqires thought: How is *tefillah* a form of worship? Isn't it the other way around? During *tefillah*, Hashem listens to *us* and responds to *our* needs.

In his magnum opus, *Chorev*, Rabbi Shimshon Raphael Hirsch observes that the root of the word *tefillah* (*peh/lamed/lamed*) doesn't mean to pray or communicate to the Divine; rather, it means to contemplate, examine, and assess. Based on this linguistic insight, some have suggested that *tefillah* is more an act of listening than speaking. Through the fixed words of the holy siddur, a philosophy of life is conveyed to the participant.

Within this paradigm, *tefillah* is an act of worship because it is an act of submission, as it implies a willingness to be influenced and shaped by the values, the priorities, the principles, and the traits of Hashem that one encounters in the sacred text. In its deepest sense, *tefillah* is not spoken but experienced in silence. It is truly a worship of the heart.

This shift in emphasis from communication to contemplation is captured in the following statement about *tefillah* made by the *Rambam*:

> Any *tefillah* that lacks the proper focus, is not considered "*tefillah*."
>
> What is the proper focus?

---

1   *Devarim* 6:13 and 13:5.
2   *Devarim* 11:13.
3   *Mishneh Torah*, The Laws of Prayer 1:1.

> *That the individual removes from his mind all other thoughts, and sees himself as if he is standing before the Presence of Hashem.*[4]

Rav Chaim Soloveitchik explains that this demand is not a simple formalistic prerequisite; it is the definition of *tefillah*. If the participant is distracted and does not see himself as standing before the Presence of Hashem, his performance is not considered an "act of *tefillah*."[5] What emerges is that, at its core, *tefillah* is less about communication and more about a state of mind.

Perhaps, it is for this reason the Torah remains silent about Yosef's verbal communications with Hashem. Knowing all that we do about his greatness, it is clear Yosef davens. Yet, the Torah intentionally creates this conspicuous silence surrounding his *tefillah* in order to capture and convey the essence of Yosef's type of *tefillah*: the silent mindfulness of Hashem's presence.

Amazingly, Yosef's paradigm of *tefillah* has a sweeping impact on everything he does and says. Having taken the time out during each day to imagine himself in Hashem's presence and to contemplate His character and values, Yosef engages the world, its citizens, and all it has to offer with an ever-present awareness of Hashem. In almost every recorded remark Yosef makes in this *parashah*, Hashem is at the center:

- "Yosef answered Pharaoh, saying, 'That is beyond me; it is **G-d** Who will respond with Pharaoh's welfare.'"[6]
- "Yosef said to Pharaoh, 'The dream of Pharaoh is a single one; what **G-d** is about to do, He has told to Pharaoh.'"[7]
- "It is this matter that I have spoken to Pharaoh; What **G-d** is about to do He has shown to Pharaoh."[8]

---

4   *Mishneh Torah*, The Laws of Prayer 4:1.
5   Chaim Soloveitchik, *Expositions on the Rambam*, The Laws of Prayer 4:1.
6   *Bereishis* 41:16.
7   Ibid. 41:25.
8   Ibid. 41:28.

- "Yosef called the name of the firstborn 'Menasheh' for '**G-d** has made me forget all my hardship and all my father's household.'"[9]
- "And the name of the second he called 'Ephraim' for, '**G-d** has made me fruitful in the land of my suffering.'"[10]
- "Yosef said to them on the third day, 'Do this and live; I fear **G-d**.'"[11]

Yosef's conception of Hashem as the ultimate force behind all human activity implies a certain habit of *tefillah*. Yosef's integrated worldview, which is the source of Yosef's resilience, resolve, and ambition, is a product of his habit of *tefillah*. If you daven like the *Rambam*, you *think* and *speak* like Yosef.

Many explanations have been given as to why *parashas Mikeitz* and Chanukah almost always coincide. Perhaps we can add that what connects the two stories is fortitude, the ability to have the courage and determination to succeed, even against all odds. Only individuals implicitly aware of Hashem's abiding presence can muster the inner strength to overcome the degree of adversity the *Chashmonayim* had to face.

To this day, the medium of *tefillah*, which is not only communicative but contemplative, is a source of strength. By developing an implicit and abiding awareness of Hashem's presence we can overcome our personal and national challenges, and achieve our personal and national ambitions.

---

9   Ibid. 41:51.
10 Ibid. 41:52.
11 Ibid. 42:18.

Vayigash

A (Not So) Different Kind of Shema

WHEN YOSEF FINALLY reunites with his beloved father, after not having seen him for over two decades, he falls on his father's neck and weeps uncontrollably. To our surprise, Yaakov Avinu doesn't react in kind; he doesn't lose himself in his son's embrace. Instead, our sages inform us, Yaakov is preoccupied with the *Shema Yisrael*. The commentators famously ask: If it was the proper time to fulfill a religious obligation, why didn't Yosef feel compelled to recite the *Shema* as well? On the other hand, if doing so wasn't pressing at this moment, why was Yaakov absorbed in anything other than greeting his long-lost son?

To appreciate Yaakov's reaction upon beholding Yosef after so many years we need to first undertake a typology of the *Shema Yisrael*.

There are two general ways to classify the *Shema Yisrael*: the formal and informal:

- Within the formal paradigm, the ritual of *Shema* is a ceremony akin to a pledge of allegiance declared by all citizens of a polity. Like a pledge of allegiance, it is fixed and objective. It is fixed in that it is preordained, to be said at a set time and in a set manner by everyone. It is objective in that, regardless of one's religious temperament at the moment, it must be recited. That *Shema* can be seen as a formal acceptance of Hashem's sovereignty is reflected by positions in the Gemara that bound the recital of *Shema* with various specifications. According to these opinions, not only must *Shema* be recited at fixed times, but in a fixed posture: in the evening, lying down; in the morning, standing erect.[1] The *Shema* must be declared in *Lashon HaKodesh*,[2] our official national language, and done so audibly.[3]
- The second type of Shema is, by contrast, unceremonious. It is subjective and unrehearsed. Instead of fulfilling a shared duty, the words *Shema Yisrael Hashem Elokeinu Hashem Echad*[4] express the speaker's perception of the world. This declaration of *Shema* is less a citizen's pledge of allegiance than a personal interpretation. Moved by a turn of events, the individual is able to make sense of his life, as he grasps and experiences the oneness of it all. Naturally, he declares, Hashem is One; everything is one.

The *Shema* that Yaakov Avinu recites upon seeing Yosef, says the *Maharil Diskin*, is of the second category. Having grieved the profound loss of Yosef, only to see him now as viceroy of Egypt and savior of not only his family but of their civilization, Yaakov experiences the oneness of it all. Yaakov finally grasps — what Yosef already knows — that all the bad, all the suffering, was by design and for their ultimate good. When

---

1 BT *Berachos* 10b.
2 BT *Berachos* 13a.
3 BT *Berachos* 15a.
4 *Devarim* 6:4.

Yaakov declares, "*Shema Yisrael Hashem Elokeinu Hashem Echad,*" he is not discharging any formal duty but expressing his newfound perception.[5]

In the final analysis, our daily *Shema* is not simply of the pure formal type, but a blend of both categories:

- On the one hand, it must be recited at prescribed times, irrespective of one's mood.
- On the other hand, the *Shema Yisrael* is subjective. It can be recited in any posture one prefers.[6] And although ideally it should be declared in *Lashon HaKodesh* and made audible, any language one understands suffices — even when done barely at a whisper.[7] In pressing circumstances, merely contemplating the words is also enough.[8]

That *Shema* is a hybrid, a mixture of ceremony and informality, is not lost on the midrash. Based on the *Shema*'s unique set of guidelines, our sages feel compelled to contrast a mortal king's royal proclamations that must be announced publically and with pomp and circumstance, with Hashem's royal proclamation — the recitation of the *Shema* — which can be declared with less fanfare and fuss.[9]

The *Shema* balances the objective and subjective, the formal and the casual, the fixed and spontaneous, because it demands obedience to Hashem while at the same time nurturing a genuine worldview. Over time, through the recitation of the hybrid *Shema*, the Torah envisions that the individual will develop a sweeping perspective informed by the Oneness of Hashem and the oneness of the world.

This goal of the hybrid *Shema* is reflected in the speech delivered by the designated *Kohen* to soldiers heading to battle:

> *Hear, O Israel: You approach today to do battle against your enemies. Do not be fainthearted. Do not fear, and do not tremble*

---

5 Commentary to *Bereishis* 46:29.
6 *Shulchan Aruch* 63:1.
7 Ibid. 62:2–3, and see *Mishnah Berurah* ibid.
8 Ibid. 62:4.
9 *Pesikta deRav KaHana* 9:5.

or be terrified because of them. For Hashem, your G-d, He goes with you, to fight for you against your enemies, to save you.[10]

As *Rashi* explains, the superfluity of the opening phrase "*Shema Yisrael*" alludes to the promise that even if all the soldiers have is the merit of the *Shema* alone, it is enough to save them. Rabbi Dr. Richard Weiss of the Young Israel of Hillcrest, explains that sometimes in the course of life, such as at war, there will be no time for rituals and ceremonies. However, what will always endure are the values and principles reflected in those rituals and ceremonies. Unable to perform even the ritual of *Shema*, the Jewish soldier can rely on his unique perception of the world and its events to get him through. Armed with the *Shema's* distilled message that Hashem is One and everything is one, the Jewish soldier need not fear.

Due to the *Shema Yisrael* we are equipped to face life's routine challenges and unexpected hurdles. Our twice-daily pledge of allegiance to Hashem, with its shades of informality and subjectivity, simultaneously strengthens our commitment to Hashem and enriches our personal understanding of His world.

---

10   *Devarim* 20:3–4.

Vayechi

From Rags to Riches

BEFORE HE DIES, Yosef brings his two sons before his father to be given a *berachah*. Among the *berachos* that they receive, Yaakov Avinu famously blesses them, "By you shall Israel bless saying, 'May G-d make you like Ephraim and Menasheh.'"[1] Although this has been our practice ever since, we shouldn't take it for granted. As a people, we don't suffer from a dearth of heroes. From Avraham Avinu to Moshe Rabbeinu to David HaMelech, our history is marked by transcendent and epic personalities. Why in particular, are Ephraim and Menasheh singled out? Why, for all time, is our hope for our children to be like them?

As one would expect, a number of answers have been offered to resolve this dilemma:

---

1   *Bereishis* 48:20.

- Some suggest that, unlike the tandem of Yitzchak and Yishmael, Yaakov and Eisav, and Yaakov's twelve sons, Ephraim and Menasheh are the first set of brothers that don't experience conflict and competition. We bless our children to be like Ephraim and Menasheh in the hope of realizing a lasting unity within our people.
- Others suggest that since it is our destiny to be in exile for so long, with its concomitant high risk of assimilation, it is only fitting that we bless our children to be able to retain their Jewish identity and remain faithful to Hashem the same way Ephraim and Menasheh had done, despite growing up in the alien culture of Egypt.

In addition to these classic explanations, let us suggest a third reason behind this timeless *berachah*. In order to do so, we need to go back to when Yosef first named his boys.

In *parashas Mikeitz*, Yosef names his firstborn Menasheh, "because G-d has made me forget all my hardship and all my father's household."[2] The logic, however, behind this name is somewhat flawed. If Yosef is truly grateful for having forgotten his troubled past, why does he choose a name that is, albeit indirectly, a constant reminder of those very hardships? Moreover, the rationale for his first son's name is inconsistent with his own expressed thoughts at the naming of his second son. Yosef calls his second son Ephraim, "for G-d has made me fruitful in the land of my suffering."[3] By expressing his gratitude for having forgotten his father's household with the name "Menasheh," Yosef indicates a sense of satisfaction with his new home, Egypt. Yet, when Yosef names Ephraim, he refers to Egypt as "the land of my suffering." Which one is it? Does or doesn't he want to forget his difficult past? Is Yosef indeed happy in Egypt or would he rather be with his father's household?

---

2 Ibid. 41:51. The name "Menasheh" is linguistically derived from the Hebrew root word *nun/shin/hei* which means "to forget."

3 Ibid. 41:52. The name "Ephraim" is linguistically derived from the Hebrew root word *peh/reish/hei* which means "to bear fruit."

There is a moving story of unwavering *emunah* that took place during the Spanish expulsion, as told by the Jewish historian, Solomon Ibn Verga, who lived through and chronicled the events of the Spanish expulsion:

> *I heard from some of the elders who came out of Spain that one of the boats was infested with the plague, and the captain of the boat put the passengers ashore at some uninhabited place. And there most of them died of starvation, while some of them gathered up all their strength to set out on foot in search of some settlement.*
>
> *There was one Jew among them who struggled on afoot together with his wife and two children. The wife grew faint and died, because she was not accustomed to so much difficult walking. The husband carried his children along until both he and they fainted from hunger. When he regained consciousness, he found that his two children had died.*
>
> *In great grief he rose to his feet and said, "O Lord of all the universe, You are doing a great deal that I might even desert my faith. But know You of certainty that — even against the will of heaven — a Jew I am and a Jew I shall remain. And neither that which You have brought upon me nor that which You will yet bring upon me will be of no avail."*
>
> *Thereupon he gathered some earth and some grass, and covered the boys, and went forth in search of a settlement.*[4]

What appears to be a moving monologue is, in fact, only one side of an ongoing dialogue. Despite personal and collective suffering, this anonymous Jew remains steadfast in his faith and capable of a heartfelt conversation with Hashem. Sometimes, however, the opposite

---

4   Cited in Jonathan Sacks, *To Heal a Fractured World: The Ethics of Responsibility* (Schocken Books, 2005), pp.198–9.

conversation must take place between an individual and Hashem. For it is not only hardship and misfortune that can cause an individual to desert Hashem, but success.

Based on the information provided to us by the text at the time Yosef names his boys, we can reconstruct and imagine the following conversation between him and Hashem:

> '*Menasheh*': O Lord of all the universe, You are doing a great deal that I might even desert my faith: You have made me viceroy over Egypt and granted me two wonderful boys; You have given me success and glory to such a degree that it would be easy for me to forget my father's household, to forget my heritage, to forget even You, Hashem.
>
> But know You of certainty that — even against the will of heaven — '*Ephraim!*': I still consider Egypt the land of my sufferings, for a Jew I am and a Jew I shall remain! I shall always remember You, Hashem, the Source of my proliferation and my good fortune.

Having climbed out of the dregs of society only to swiftly reach the apex of Egyptian society, Yosef is at risk of forgetting not only his one-time struggles, but Hashem — the source of his success. The greatness of Yosef, then, is his loyalty to Hashem and his father's tradition despite his overwhelming success.

Many contemporary commentators see *Sefer Devarim* as one long warning against the spiritual dangers of personal and national success. In *Sefer Devarim*, Moshe Rabbeinu's intended audience is not a collection of religiously minded individuals, but a nation under G-d, with a land, a government, and the means to support and defend itself. Consequently, Moshe warns the people repeatedly "not to forget Hashem"[5] and misattribute their achievements to

---

5   *Devarim* 8:11.

their "own strength and might."[6] This recurring theme leads Rabbi Jonathan Sacks to say that for the Jewish people:

> *The greatest challenge is not slavery but freedom; not poverty but affluence; not danger but security; not homelessness but home. The paradox is that when we have most to thank G-d for, that is when we are in greatest danger of not thanking — nor even thinking of — G-d at all.*[7]

Whether we are sovereign over our own land or dispersed throughout the globe in modern liberal democracies, we are vulnerable to the spiritual pitfalls of success. Social acceptance breeds contentment and achievement begets arrogance. When we bless our children to be like Ephraim and Menasheh, we join in Yosef's dialogue with Hashem. By doing so, we bless our children to see not only success, but to do so while remaining mindful of Hashem and His ultimate hope for us.

May you be like Ephraim and Menasheh.

---

6   Ibid. 8:17.
7   Jonathan Sacks (Aug. 2007). "Judaism's Greatest Challenge," Covenant & Conversation. Retrieved from http://rabbisacks.org/ki-tavo-5767-judaism-greatest-challenge/

Blessings and Brexit

NOT TOO LONG ago, the George Washington Presidential Inaugural Bible was on display. On April 30, 1789, George Washington placed his hand on this Bible and took the oath of office, becoming the first president of the United States. For the exhibit, the Bible was open to the actual page on which Washington placed his hand: chapters 49 and 50 of Genesis.

Perhaps President Washington chose to rest his hand on the portion containing Yaakov Avinu's blessings to each of the *Shevatim* while on his deathbed, because as he was about to assume the leadership of a nascent nation, he identified with Yaakov Avinu's concerns and anxieties. Hoping to draw inspiration and blessing for himself and his nation, Washington invokes Yaakov's blessings.

The fledgling nation Washington was about to lead was not comprised of a homogeneous people, with one character and one culture, led by one body of government and constitution. Instead, America was a federation, a two-tiered government, whereby power is shared between an overarching national government and regional governments. In this conglomeration, each of the thirteen original states not only had its own government and constitution, but its own distinct character and culture. In fact, many states, particularly in the south, still viewed the newly constituted union as nothing more than a confederation, a loose collection of separate sovereign states that have not relinquished any significant power. And more than power was at stake, so was identity.

Constituted as a federation, the newly formed American national government had to compete with the variegated states for the hearts and minds of the people. The tension that existed between the national and state governments was not only over executive and legislative power, but over identity formation. Would each citizen identify first and foremost as an "American" or as a member of their respective state? Would a citizen of Virginia want to be recognized and known as an "American" first and a "Virginian" second, or vice versa? And, if forced to choose, where would their loyalties lie? As Washington began his presidency, the answers to these questions were not yet known.

Almost eight years later, in 1796, these tensions and their possible outcomes still preoccupied Washington, and they were the talking points of his farewell address. Believing that their happiness was contingent on their union, Washington, while downplaying their differences, implored the people to remain united and to primarily self-identify by their national name:

> *The name of "American," which belongs to you in your national capacity, must always exalt the just pride of patriotism more than any designation derived from local differences. With slight shades of difference, you have the same religion, manners, habits, and political principles.*

Similar tensions and competing loyalties preoccupied Yaakov Avinu, too, as he bid farewell. For the sundry *Shevatim* were destined to be neither a loose confederation of tribes nor a homogenized, uniform nation, but a federation.

In *parashas Vayishlach*, after Yaakov had successfully confronted both the angel and Eisav, Hashem changes his name to "Yisrael" and blesses him: "Be fruitful and multiply; a nation (*goy*) and a community of nations (*kahal goyim*) shall come into being from you."[1] That Yaakov is promised that he will be both a "nation" and a "community of nations" implies that Am Yisrael is to be organized as a federation, a two-tiered existence, whereby each *shevet* is viewed as a subnation within a larger, overarching nation. As Rav Shimshon Raphael Hirsch explains:

---

1 *Bereishis* 35:11.

> *The nation that will descend from him is to be, in its external relations one single unit (goy), and internally a united congregation of many kinds of people and professions (kehal goyim).*[2]

Not unlike the United States of America, Israel will be led on two levels:

- On the national level, the country will be led by the king and the national Supreme Court (comprised of the seventy-one greatest sages of the nation).
- On the *shevet* level, each *shevet* will be led by its *nasi* and regional Supreme Court (comprised of the twenty-three greatest sages of the *shevet*).[3] Like the states, each *shevet* has its own territorial integrity, as well as its own flag, representing its unique character and culture. This is so because within the framework of Am Yisrael, each *shevet* is meant to retain its individuality. As Rav Shimshon Raphael Hirsch continues,

> *Each shevet is to represent a special national quality; each shevet is to be, as it were, a nation in miniature. In its tribes, martial nations as well as merchant ones, agricultural nations as well as scientific and scholarly ones, are all to be represented.*[4]

With a shared sense of purpose and destiny, each *shevet* is meant to contribute its unique perspective, character, and talents to aid in the administration of the nation. And on an individual level, each citizen in the polity is to identify both with the nation, Israel, and with his respective *shevet*.

Because the *Shevatim* are destined to preserve their distinctiveness within a "community of nations," Yaakov Avinu blesses each one of them individually, highlighting their respective strengths and weaknesses. But because the *Shevatim* are also destined to constitute a whole

---

2   Commentary to ibid.
3   See *Ramban* in his commentary to *Devarim* 16:18.
4   Ibid.

"nation," while preserving their respective character, he blesses them in the presence of one another, as a group. That the *Shevatim* will function as a federation, with each *shevet* contributing to the national welfare while retaining its integrity, is alluded to by the Torah when it describes that, when Yaakov blessed the *Shevatim*, "each in accordance with what was his special blessing, did he bless them."[5] The midrash explains that the Torah switches from the singular ("his") to the plural ("them") in order to convey that although Yaakov singles out each *shevet*'s unique qualities, all the *Shevatim* will draw and benefit from one another. Even though each *shevet* will receive a defined territory with unique natural resources, all the *Shevatim* will share with one another.[6]

Still, as we have seen, there is an inherent tension in a federation between the national and regional level over issues of power and identity. Because in a federation each region is encouraged to preserve its individuality, there exists an inherent vulnerability for competition, conflict, betrayals, and indifference. Their lack of uniformity makes them vulnerable to disunity. Instead of working together for the sake of the national enterprise, their differences could drive the *Shevatim* apart. For this reason, Yaakov's farewell message was to form and maintain a union. On his deathbed, Yaakov calls his sons and says, "Come together…Assemble yourselves and listen, O sons of Yaakov, and listen to Israel your father."[7] The midrash, noticing how Yaakov stresses and emphasizes that his sons gather together, infers that "Yaakov commanded them regarding factionalism and conflict. He said to them, be one unit."[8]

Unfortunately, Yaakov's message goes unheeded. Am Yisrael's early history in Eretz Yisrael, as depicted in *Sefer Shoftim*, is characterized by intertribal competition, conflict, betrayal, and indifference. There is not one, but two civil wars. No *shofet* is able to unify the people. No one

---

5   Bereishis 49:28.
6   Cited in Menachem Kasher, *Torah Shelemah: Volume VII* (The Torah Shelemah Institute, 1992), p. 1,858.
7   Ibid. 49:1–2.
8   *Bereishis Rabbah* 98:2.

even comes close. And, ultimately, the entrenched differences between the *Shevatim* lead to a schism, resulting in two separate kingdoms, as depicted in *Sefer Melachim*.

It was no accident of birth that Yaakov Avinu has twelve worthy sons, from four different mothers, raised by two different matriarchs. This was all by Divine design. Am Yisrael is not meant to be a simple, homogenous nation, characterized by uniformity. Rather, Am Yisrael is meant to be a federation, a complex political system, characterized by diversity.

Cultural diversity, however, often leads to dissension, indifference, and disunity. While this possible outcome poses a challenge, to secure unity at the expense of tribal diversity would be considered a failure no less than perpetual discord. This, therefore, is the unique challenge for the members of Am Yisrael: to achieve unity without uniformity. It is the challenge given by Yaakov to his sons. It is the challenge that still lies before us. And, ultimately, it is the challenge that faces humanity.

According to Rav Hirsch, the reason Hashem designed Am Yisrael as a complex federation was for it to serve as a model for all nations of the world:

> *Thus the fact is to be made clear to the world that the devotion and sanctification of human life in the bond with G-d, through His Law, is not dependent on or conditional to any special calling in life or national characteristic. But that the whole of mankind, with all its diversity is called on to accept the one common conception of G-d, as taught by Israel, and so form all the different individual and national characteristics of mankind into one united kingdom of G-d.*[9]

With Am Yisrael as its precedent, the Torah envisions that one day all the nations of the world will unite to form a federation under Hashem. Sadly, as both Jewish and modern world history have shown us, achieving unity without uniformity does not come easy. When nations see

---

9   Commentary to *Bereishis* 35:11. See also his commentary to *Bereishis* 48:3.

themselves as separate entities with unique histories and cultures, they are predisposed to emphasize their differences over their shared similarities. Their diversity, instead of being seen as a catalyst for collective creativity, drives them apart and incites antagonism.

As a reaction to all the bloodshed of the first half of the twentieth century caused by extreme nationalism, the European Union (EU) was formed. Ever since, there has been a push among many European intellectuals toward a unification of humanity. By doing away with borders, citizenship, and nations, they hope to achieve everlasting peace. For this reason, Britain's choice to leave the EU sparked such fury. Any expression of nationalistic aspirations is seen by universalists as an obstacle to peace and a precursor to war.

However, if a worldwide federation is what Hashem envisions for the nations of the world, then securing perpetual peace at the expense of national independence and diversity is considered a failure no less than perpetual discord. In this light, Brexit was a move in the right direction. It served the EU notice that genuine peace is not achieved by compelling nations to commit what is tantamount to national suicide. Rather, a balance between healthy nationalism and wanting to live in a global community is the prerequisite for genuine peace.

The precedent of Am Yisrael's federation, as articulated by Rav Hirsch, implies that the only factor that can truly unify the diverse nations of the world as a global community without homogenizing them is the universal acceptance of Hashem's sovereignty. Only then, when the sundry nations of the world organize themselves as a federation under Hashem, will genuine peace be secured, forever.

Shemos

The Parashah with No Names

ALTHOUGH THE MIDRASH records that Moshe Rabbeinu was given various names at birth by the different members of his immediate family,[1] it is "Moshe," the name given to him by the daughter of Pharaoh, that Hashem Himself uses, exclusively. Why is the name Moshe, given to him by Pharaoh's daughter, given preference over all the others, and why does it endure for all time?

Furthermore, while we are on the subject of names, Rabbi Yitzchak Aramah, in his classic work *Akeidas Yitzchak*, is troubled why *parashas Shemos* begins by listing the names of Yaakov Avinu's sons who accompanied him down to Egypt; information we already know. Why the redundancy?

The *Encyclopedia of Genocide*, in the entry "Adolf Eichmann,"

---

1   *Vayikra Rabbah* 1:3.

under the subtitle "Psychology of Adolf Eichmann," records that during the course of his imprisonment in Israel, Eichmann was thoroughly examined and given extensive psychological testing by the husband-wife psychiatrist-psychologist team of Drs. Shlomo and Shoshana Kulcsar. The findings of their studies emphasized Eichmann's "inability to experience humanness — connection and feeling for people. People were organized as *things* for him." Their findings about Eichmann are

> *consistent with a great deal of other evidence in psychology that one major group of killers and destroyers in everyday human life involves people who do not experience the humanness of others, but who treat others as things or instruments serving whatever needs, obligations, or ambitions that are important to them. Psychologist George Bach suggested the concept thinging.*[2]

With this psychological phenomenon in mind, we can suggest that the Torah repeats the names of the sons of Yaakov to emphasize that the rest of the narrative, which describes the enslavement and living conditions of the Jewish people in Egypt, contains *no* names. The Torah records that "a man of the house of Levi went and took a daughter of Levi,"[3] without telling us their names. When this anonymous couple conceive and have a son, we are not told the child's name. And when the baby's sister watches over him from the river's bank, again, we are not told the name of this brave girl. It seems that the Torah intentionally leaves out their names to reflect the Egyptians' perception of the Jewish people. The Egyptians dehumanized the Jewish people and perceived them as *things* — as objects with no names — making it easier to manipulate and victimize them.

It is true, we do encounter in the course of the narrative Jewish

---

2   Israel W. Charny, *Encyclopedia of Genocide: Volume I* (ABC-CLIO, 1999), p. 210.
3   *Shemos* 2:1.

personalities with names: the Jewish midwives, Shifrah and Puah. However, these are not their real names. Rather, these names, as *Rashi* says, are descriptions of the function they perform:

> [Her real name] is Yocheved; she is called Shifrah because she beautifies the child at birth. [Her real name] is Miriam; she is called Puah because she cries, and speaks, and coos to the child in the manner of women who soothe a crying baby.⁴

Calling Yocheved "Shifrah" is equivalent to calling your mechanic (whose real name is Paul), "Tune-up." Greeting Miriam in the morning with, "Good morning, Puah," is equivalent to walking into your local supermarket and greeting Susan, the lady at the register, "Good morning, Check-out." Instead of real names, "Shifrah" and "Puah" are simply labels assigned to Yocheved and Miriam by Pharaoh in an attempt to strip them of their identity and dehumanize them. This is the meaning of the otherwise obscure *pasuk*:

> The king of Egypt said to the Hebrew midwives, of whom the name of the first was Shifrah and the name of the second was Puah. And he said, "When you deliver the Hebrew women, and you see them on the birthstool; if it is a son, you are to kill him, and if it is a daughter, she shall live."⁵

What exactly does Pharaoh say to Shifrah and Puah initially? The instruction to kill all the newborn boys is an additional remark ("and he said") to the initial statement ("The king of Egypt said"). Ostensibly, what was originally said is left to the imagination. According to a Chassidic tradition, however, what Pharaoh says to them initially is in fact explicit in the *pasuk*. What Pharaoh says — what he demands — is that the midwives, Yocheved and Miriam, no longer be called by their personal names, but by the service they provide. According to this

---

4   Commentary to *Shemos* 1:15.
5   *Shemos* 1:15–16.

interpretation, the *pasuk* should read like this: "And the King of Egypt said to the Hebrew midwives that the name of one shall be 'Shifrah' and the name of the second shall be 'Puah.'" The Egyptians, led by Pharaoh, are guilty of *thinging*: they do not experience the "humanness" of the Jewish people. To the Egyptians, the Jews are nameless things.

It is no surprise, therefore, that for almost two centuries, no individual arises out of the Jewish multitude to lead the people to freedom. In Egypt, the Jewish people internalize the way they are perceived and treated by the ruling class: as things. Dehumanized, the Jewish people lack the necessary self-esteem, confidence, and initiative to stand up to their masters. Only someone who is able to see himself as an individual with a name — as a person and not as a thing — has the capacity to resist and overcome his oppressors. This truism is illustrated poignantly in the following story.

Bruno Bettelheim, the Austrian-born psychologist who spent almost a year in the concentration camps of Dachau and Buchenwald, tells a story of a concentration camp inmate. The SS had gathered a group of prisoners and lined them up to enter the gas chamber. The SS commanding officer, learning that one of the female prisoners had been a professional dancer, demanded that she perform and dance before him. As the woman danced before the officer, she maneuvered herself close enough to him to be able to grab his gun from his holster, and she shot him dead on the spot. Of course, she was killed instantaneously, as she was riddled with bullets by the other SS men on the scene. Bruno Bettelheim had this to say:

> *Isn't it probable that despite the grotesque setting in which she danced, dancing made her once again a person. Dancing, she was singled out as an individual, asked to perform in what had once been her chosen vocation. No longer was she a number, a nameless depersonalized prisoner, but the dancer she used to be. Transformed however momentarily, she responded like her old self, destroying the enemy bent on her destruction even if she had to die in the process.*[6]

---

6   Bruno Bettelheim, *The Informed Heart: Autonomy in a Mass Age* (Penguin, 1991), pp. 258-9.

In Egypt, as in Nazi-occupied Europe, the Jewish people are reduced to things and, for almost two centuries, no Jew is ever singled out as an individual, as a person with a name. Until, that is, one young woman comes along and changes everything: "And [the daughter of Pharaoh] called his name Moshe, and said: 'Because I drew him out of the water.'"[7]

During the course of their enslavement, Moshe is the first and only Jew to be called by a proper name by an Egyptian. The daughter of Pharaoh sees in the baby she finds, not a thing, but a human being, deserving of attention, compassion, and love. By sacrificing for Moshe, taking him into the palace with her, and conferring upon him a name, she singles him out as a person. Out of all the Jewish people enslaved in Egypt, it is only Moshe who does not see himself as "a number, a nameless depersonalized" thing. It is for this reason that Moshe is able to develop the psychological tools necessary to redeem his people and it is for this reason that, of all his other names, it is the name "Moshe," given to him by the princess of Egypt, which endures for all time.

On a smaller and milder scale, it is not uncommon for us to perceive other people as things. Whenever we treat someone as a means to our ends, we are guilty of *thinging*. If when dealing with a waiter, mechanic, secretary, or cashier, we find ourselves more readily impatient or irritable than usual, it is a telltale sign that we don't truly see the provider as a person. In such scenarios, it behooves us to remind ourselves that this individual is a son, a mother, a wife, who may have other, more important or urgent things on his or her mind. Maybe he just came back from visiting his loved one in the hospital. Or maybe she is stressed over how she is going to pay the rent. Or maybe he is just having a bad day; it happens to us all. When we relate to such individuals, may we be conscious of the fact that they are real people and that our interactions with them are between two fellow human beings. Not between us and a thing.

---

7   *Shemos* 2:10.

Dancing Children

ACCORDING TO OUR sages, Amram, the future father of Moshe Rabbeinu, is the undisputed leader of the Jewish people in Egypt when Pharaoh decrees that all newborn boys be drowned in the Nile. So when Amram divorces his wife in response to Pharaoh's evil decree, the rest of the men follow suit and divorce theirs. Upon witnessing the breakup of all these families and the concomitant lost potential for future children, Miriam confronts her father and successfully persuades him to reconsider. When Amram remarries his wife, the rest of the men do so as well.[1]

Because the Torah doesn't stress that Amram "took her *back*," and instead employs the regular expression for marriage, "and he took her,"[2] our sages infer that their remarriage was marked and celebrated as if it was their first. In the sages' reconstruction, Yocheved is placed under a canopy, and both Miriam and Aharon dance and rejoice before her.

The *Ramban* is bothered how Aharon, who was a mere toddler at the time, could have appreciated the significance of the event. He offers two solutions:

- Either Miriam coached Aharon, and he just mimicked her, as little siblings are wont to do;
- Or, Hashem inspired Aharon.

While the first answer is unremarkable, the second is extraordinary. Divine intervention should not be taken for granted; it is no small thing.

---

1 BT *Sotah* 12a.
2 *Shemos* 2:1.

Why, then, does Hashem get involved? What is so important about the wedding ceremony that Aharon needed to participate in it?

Amram's course of action in response to Pharaoh's evil decree isn't the only policy he establishes as communal leader in Egypt. When the *Ramham* discusses the Seven Noachide Laws, he introduces them as the first installment of a larger code that developed over time. In Gan Eden, Adam HaRishon is commanded to observe six commandments. Generations later, Noach receives the seventh. Until Avraham Avinu emerges on the scene, the set of laws regulating ethical monotheism remain static. With Avraham, a gradual expansion of the laws recommences, only to climax at Har Sinai:

> *When Avraham arose, in addition to these, he was commanded regarding circumcision. He also ordained the morning prayers. Yitzchak separated tithes and ordained an additional prayer service before sunset. Yaakov added the prohibition against eating the sciatic nerve. He also ordained the evening prayers. In Egypt, Amram was commanded regarding other mitzvos. Ultimately, Moshe came and the Torah was completed by him.*[3]

In contrast to the contribution of the Avos, the *Rambam* does not explain which mitzvos Amram legislates. While many of the classic commentators leave the issue unresolved, some posit, based on the Gemara cited earlier, that what Amram adds to the growing list are the mitzvos of *kiddushin* and *gerushin*, the Jewish laws of marriage and divorce.[4] What remains to be seen, however, is why are these institutions introduced now, at this point in Jewish history? Circumcision both signifies and creates the covenant. Daily *tefillah* structures our day and encourages constant communication with Hashem. And the prohibition of the sciatic nerve memorializes the family's triumph over adversity. Why, though, from among the plethora of all the other

---

3 *Mishneh Torah*, The Laws of Kings 9:1.
4 Cited in *Sefer HaLikutim* to *Mishneh Torah*, ibid.

mitzvos, is *kiddushin* and *gerushin* added so early in Jewish history, a century before the Sinaitic Revelation? And if, for some reason, these institutions are so important, why aren't they legislated by the Avos?

The answer, it seems, lies in the fact that Amram, unlike the Avos before him, is entrusted not with leading a family, but a nascent nation. For a small family, albeit one with high ambitions, a family insignia, a few customs, and raw talent, are sufficient to ensure the preservation and perpetuation of values and vision.

Amram, on the other hand, is the head of multitudes, whose birth rates are skyrocketing; very quickly, their family has grown into a fledgling nation. Because he has to deal with a massive number of people spread across a wide spectrum of talents and tendencies, he can no longer rely on symbols, rituals, and individual talent to perpetuate their family's legacy. What he needs is an institutionalized social mechanism that will guarantee the transmission of their values and vision from generation to generation. He finds what he is looking for in the mitzvos of *kiddushin* and *gerushin*.

The *Rambam* introduces the mitzvah and laws of *kiddushin* as follows:

> *Before the Torah was given, when a man would meet a woman in the marketplace and he and she decided to marry, he would bring her home, conduct relations in private and thus make her his wife. [The woman is considered divorced when her husband removes her from his home and sends her on her own or when she leaves his domain and goes her own way. They have no written divorce proceedings. Whenever he or she decides to separate, they may and then are no longer considered as married.[5]]*
>
> *Once the Torah was given, the Jews were commanded that when a man desires to marry a woman, he must acquire her as a wife in the presence of witnesses. [Only] after this, does she become his wife...This process of acquisition is universally*

---

5   Mishneh Torah, The Laws of Kings 9:8.

referred to as erusin or kiddushin. Once this process of acquisition has been formalized and a woman has become mekudeshes...if her husband desires to divorce her, he must compose a get (bill of divorce).[6]

Why does the *Rambam*, in his law code, give us a history lesson? My *rebbi*, Rabbi Michael Rosensweig, explains that the *Rambam* is highlighting the Torah's unique contribution to the institution of marriage. By requiring the ceremonious act of *kiddushin* before the consummation of the marriage (*nisuin*), and written divorce proceedings upon its dissolution, the Torah has redefined marriage. No longer is marriage an intense form of companionship — an inherently casual and temporary relationship, wherein the participants enter the relationship with the attitude that they are not making a permanent commitment, and that splitting up and moving on to someone more appealing is as viable an option as staying together. Instead, the type of marriage the Torah envisions is a permanent relationship, as reflected in the formal way it is both created and terminated, if absolutely necessary.

To be sure, this orientation of permanence allows the couple to maximize their potential for meaningful happiness, as it makes them a union and creates an abiding framework to raise a family together, both of which are satisfying and fulfilling. But the Torah's main objective behind permanent marriage is even more ambitious, and it is there where its real interests lie: the faithful transmission of Torah values and vision from generation to generation, across the socioeconomic spectrum. The stability and security inherent in permanent marriage creates an environment conducive to raising and educating healthy and well-adjusted children, who will, in all likelihood, pass on the way of life they have received to the next generation. For this reason, observes Rabbi Rosensweig, the *Rambam* enjoins a man to fulfill his mitzvah of procreation not with just any woman, but with "her"[7] — the woman

---

6   *Mishneh Torah*, The Laws of Marriage 1:1.
7   Ibid., in his introductory remarks to The Laws of Marriage.

he has performed *kiddushin* with. In order to maximize his offspring's potential, he is to raise and educate them in a stable, wholesome environment.

We live in a culture that is increasingly ignoring the contribution of *kiddushin* and *gerushin* to society. Living in our religious and somewhat insular communities, we do not always fully appreciate the extent of the cavalier attitude many people in American society have toward the institution of marriage. With the no-fault divorce legislation that swept the country from state to state in the 1970s, one out of every two marriages now end in divorce.

Paralleling the rise in divorce rates, alternatives to marriage, such as cohabitation, whereby couples live together without legalizing their marriage, have become more popular. In 1970, there were five hundred thousand cohabitating couples in this country; currently, there are over five million. Taken together, children in today's age are born and raised in radically different circumstances than in previous generations. As of 2013, the rate of all births in America born to unmarried women was forty percent. And one out of ten American women have had three or more live-in partners (husbands or otherwise) by age thirty-five. Compounding the financial and emotional hardships single mothers often suffer, the impact of such high instability can be quite negative, if not devastating for the children involved.

As a social worker, I have been witness to real-life examples of these sad statistics. One fifteen-year-old boy hadn't seen his biological father in well over a decade. He grew close to and fond of his mother's second live-in partner, the father of his ten-year old sister, only to be deeply disappointed when his mother broke up with him. When I started seeing him, his mother had recently given birth to a third child, from a third man. Without getting into the details of this client's specific situation, he stopped coming to sessions because his mother couldn't find the time to bring him. Her new family dynamic placed demands on her that, unfortunately, came at the expense of her first child, from a fleeting relationship long ago. Another client of mine was one of six children. From four separate men. The mother is in her thirties. Based on our interactions and conversations, it was evident that Mom favored her youngest child from her current husband, while she acted less than tenderly toward my client, from a previous relationship.

Clearly, children are disadvantaged when they lack stability and a sense of security, as they go from household to household, from father-figure to father-figure.

Can a child succeed despite such circumstances? Yes. Can values be transmitted in such a context? Yes. Has it been done? Yes. There are unique and exceptional individuals. But in the aggregate, when dealing with a massive population, with an entire society, it's unlikely. That's why the Torah legislates and regulates marriage. The Torah is concerned for the well-being of spouses and children, and has a vested interest in their capacity to transmit and receive, respectively, society's traditions and values. For this reason, the Torah — through the mechanisms of *kiddushin* and *gerushin* — redefines marriage as a permanent institution. And this is why Amram, at this transitional point in Jewish history, when the family transforms into a nation, institutes the mitzvos of *kiddushin* and *gerushin*.

Hashem inspires little Aharon to rejoice and dance at his parents' second wedding to make a point, and it is this: Don't think Amram and Yocheved's remarriage is only significant because of the future children they may (and will) conceive. Indeed, that's why Miriam dances. But their remarriage is also a cause for celebration because it will impact their current children. Miriam and Aharon will be healthier, happier, and more integrated because of the permanence of their parents' marriage. As a result, they will be fit to faithfully carry and transmit their parents' values and vision to the next generation. That's why Aharon dances.

Va'eira

A Visit to the Egyptian Zoo

NOT TOO LONG ago, the London Zoo hosted a special exhibit: *homo sapiens*. The exhibit, which lasted four days, displayed three male and five female homo sapiens (actual people!) next to their primate 'relatives,' separated by an electric fence. As with all zoo exhibits, a sign educated visitors about the species' diet, natural habitat, worldwide distribution, and the threats to its survival. A spokeswoman for the London Zoo, Polly Wills, explained the impetus behind the exhibit. "Seeing people in a different environment, among other animals," she said, "teaches members of the public that the human is just another primate."[1]

The group of eight was chosen from an online contest that drew thirty candidates. At the exhibit they were seen relaxing in the sun,

---

1 The Associated Press, "At London Zoo, Homo Sapiens Is Just Another Primate Species," *New York Times*, Aug. 2005.

at play with balls and hula hoops, and eating. Rest assured, they were, of course, allowed to leave and go home at closing time. One of the participants, Tom Mahoney, twenty-six, was inspired to get involved in order to generate more sympathy and support for our fellow primates. "A lot of people think humans are above other animals," Mahoney said. "When they see humans as animals, here, it kind of reminds us that we're not that special."[2]

This pervasive and pernicious view, that we are not fundamentally different than animals, is not a new one. It has plagued and hindered mankind for millennia. It's an attitude that existed in Egypt, and one expressed by Pharaoh himself. However, before we get to Pharaoh, the human at the center of the story of Egypt, Let us begin with the animals.

The fourth plague suffered by the Egyptians was *arov*, wild animals. "If you don't send My people," warns Hashem, "I will send the swarm of wild beasts (*arov*); and the houses of Egypt shall be filled with the swarm (*ha'arov*), and even the ground upon which they are."[3] The *Be'er Yosef* was bothered why Moshe uses the term "*arov*" to express the coming of wild animals. Why doesn't Moshe name the plague directly, the way he does with *dam*, *tzefardeia*, and *kinim*? Why doesn't Moshe simply warn Pharaoh that if he doesn't let the Jewish people go, Egypt will come under the attack of "*chayos ra'os* — wild beasts"?[4]

This isn't the only difference between this plague and the ones that precede it. Only here does Hashem stress that, with this plague, a clear distinction will emerge between the Egyptians and Jews:

> And on that day I shall set apart the land of Goshen upon which My people stands, that there shall be no swarm there; so that you will know that I am Hashem in the midst of the land…I shall make a distinction between My people and your people — tomorrow the sign will come about![5]

---

2 Ibid.
3 *Shemos* 8:17.
4 Commentary to ibid.
5 *Shemos* 8:18–19.

The problem with this idea is that all the previous plagues similarly differentiated and discriminated between Egyptian and Jew. Unlike the Egyptians, the Jews had untainted water to drink. No frogs pestered them. No lice infested them. There were already so many differences: Why would Hashem single out the plague of *arov* as an indicator of difference between the Egyptians and Jews?

In *parashas Bereishis*, Rav Shimshon Raphael Hirsch is bothered why Hashem designates humans with the name Adam.[6] Ostensibly, the name is linguistically derived from the word *adamah*, and since man was formed from the dust of the earth, humans are fittingly called Adam. The problem with this approach, says Rav Hirsch, is that animals, too, emerged from the *adamah*.[7] Because of this difficulty, Rav Hirsch is compelled to find some other etymological source for the word *adam*.[8] The *Netziv*, Rabbi Naftali Zvi Yehuda Berlin, however, resolves Rav Hirsch's dilemma without altering the meaning of the word *adam*.

When Hashem creates man, the Torah records, "Then Hashem, G-d, formed man out of dust from the ground."[9] *Rashi*, quoting the midrash, comments that when Hashem gathers dust from the ground to form man, He gathers it from all four corners of the earth.[10] The *Netziv* explains that the midrash is conveying a fundamental difference between man and animal: Animals are designed to inhabit a specific environment, a particular habitat. Man, on the other hand, is not limited to a specific environment. While it is true that animals were formed from the earth, each species was formed exclusively from the earth of their respective habitats. Man, in contrast, was fashioned from the earth of all the various surfaces, heights, and climates of the globe. Consequently, man, alone, is uniquely "the creature of the *adamah*," and rightfully called Adam.[11]

---

6   Bereishis 1:26.
7   Commentary to ibid.
8   Rav Hirsch traces the etymology of the name Adam (*alef/daled/mem*) to the color *adom* (*alef/daled/vav/mem*), red. As the "least broken ray of the spectrum, of the pure ray of light," *adom/Adam* represents "the nearest revelation of the divine on the earth." Ibid.
9   Bereishis 2:7.
10 Commentary to ibid.
11 Commentary to 2:7.

This fundamental distinction between man and animal can help us appreciate the uniqueness of the fourth plague, *arov*.

The *Be'er Yosef* suggests that Moshe uses the word *arov*, which literally means a mixture, to describe the plague, because the novelty of the plague was not the manipulation of wild beasts but the swarming of wild beasts, an effect created by the mixture of diverse species of animals. During *arov*, various species — the lion, polar bear, anaconda, etc. — each one needing its own distinct habitat to survive, converged on a single location, Egypt, with its unique environment only suited for particular creatures.

Hashem, though, doesn't miraculously enable the animals to survive despite Egypt's climate. Rather, the plague will affect "even the ground upon which the animals are." It is fascinating to note that when the wild animals converged on Egypt, the conditions of their natural habitat came with them. For example, ice and cold followed the polar bear and a tropical climate followed the anaconda. Not only did the wild animals ravage the population and produce, the sudden and drastic climate change destroyed the land of Egypt, too.[12]

In light of the *Netziv*'s insight above, it follows that Hashem's elaborate scheme is executed not merely to damage the land of Egypt, but to drive home a devastating message to the Egyptians and Pharaoh.

When Moshe first encounters Pharaoh and delivers Hashem's message to let His people go, Pharaoh responds, "Who is Hashem, that I should hearken to His voice to let Israel go? I know not Hashem, and moreover I will not let Israel go."[13] The midrash understands that Pharaoh's response is not only an expression of impudence, but of actual ignorance. Pharaoh, says the midrash, had a book cataloging all the known deities, but when he searched the book upon Moshe's arrival, there was no entry for Hashem.[14] Some explain the meaning of the midrash on a figurative level: Hashem is a different kind

---

12   Commentary to *Shemos* 8:17.
13   *Shemos* 5:2.
14   *Shemos Rabbah* 5:14.

of G-d, fundamentally unlike the types of deities Pharaoh's culture worshipped. If one were to catalogue all the gods into a book, for the sake of internal coherence, Hashem would be intentionally left out. Because He is conceptually different, Hashem needs His own book.

Polytheism is a system of local deities. The idolatrous Egyptians, by serving their local gods, limit themselves to a specific habitat. By doing so, they make themselves out to be like animals, no different than other primates, and divest themselves of the name "Adam." Hashem, however, is a transcendent G-d. He is One and He is everywhere. Consequently, His people who serve Him are not limited by a specific environment, but can live anywhere. His people, therefore, are truly *adam*. This fundamental distinction between us and pagans is alluded to in *Sefer Yechezkel*, which states, "Now you, My sheep, sheep of my pasture — you are Adam; I am your G-d."[15] The Gemara infers from the pronoun "you," that *only you*, Bnei Yisrael, are called Adam; pagans, however, are not called Adam.[16]

Arov is singled out as being the plague that differentiates between Egyptians and Jews because its design — the swarm and mixture of various wild animals that descended on the Egyptians, each one accompanied by the conditions of its own natural habitat — taught its victims in a vicious way, that they, indeed, were not special. They behaved like animals and, thus, were no different than them. The Jews, however, were very different.

Throughout the ages, despite the fact that we have been scattered throughout the four corners of the earth, we have survived and thrived. Every time we have had to go to and settle in some place, only to pick up again and leave to another place on the globe — from Babylon to Shushan to Berlin, to Paris, Montreal, and New York — we have demonstrated that Hashem, our G-d, is everywhere. There are shuls and *batei midrash* everywhere we have been, proof that we can maintain a close, personal, and unique relationship with our transcendent G-d,

---

15   *Sefer Yechezkel* 34:31.
16   BT *Yevamos* 61a.

anywhere. For we are Adam. We are not just another primate. We are indeed special.

The *navi*, Yechezkel, in the same *perek* quoted above, using the same imagery and metaphor of a shepherd and his flock, continues:

> For thus says my Lord, Hashem: Behold! I am here, and I shall seek out My sheep, and I will investigate them. As a shepherd tends his flock on the day that he is among his scattered sheep. so I will investigate My sheep and rescue them from all the places where they were scattered on the day of clouds and darkness. I shall bring them out from the nations and gather them from the lands and bring them to their ground. Upon good pasture I will shepherd them, and upon the heights of Israel's mountains their fold will be. There they will lie down in a good fold and upon fat pastures they will graze on the mountains of Israel.[17]

Despite being flung to all four corners of the earth, Hashem promises us that from all of our scattered places, He will gather us and bring us back to our most suitable habitat, to our homeland, the Land of Israel.

---

17   *Sefer Yechezkel* 34:11–14.

Bo

The Politics of Citizenship

IN 1795, THE United States Congress composed an "Oath of Allegiance" to be taken by immigrants as part of the process to become an American citizen. The oath reads as follows:

> *I hereby declare, on oath, that I absolutely and entirely renounce and abjure all allegiance and fidelity to any foreign prince, potentate, state, or sovereignty, of whom or which I have heretofore been a subject or citizen; that I will support and defend the Constitution and laws of the United States of America against all enemies, foreign and domestic; that I will bear true faith and allegiance to the same; that I will bear arms on behalf of the United States when required by the law; that I will perform noncombatant service in the Armed Forces of the United States when required by the law; that I will perform*

work of national importance under civilian direction when required by the law; and that I take this obligation freely, without any mental reservation or purpose of evasion; so help me G-d.

Samuel P. Huntington, in his book *Who Are We? The Challenge to America's National Identity*, summarizes the spirit of the oath to two principles: exclusivity and status. According to this, while an individual can change his citizenship, he can only be a citizen of one nation at any given time. The demand of exclusivity precludes dual citizenship. The oath also implies that citizenship is a status conferred on the individual. By undergoing citizenship, the individual assumes a new identity.[1]

These basic assumptions about citizenship continued to inform American policy into the early twentieth century. For example, the "Bancroft treaties," named after American diplomat George Bancroft who orchestrated them, and were a series of treaties between the United States and various European countries, stipulated that prior citizenship would automatically expire if and when an individual became naturalized by a different country. The purpose of these treaties was to prevent individuals from having dual citizenship.

Since their signing, however, these treaties have been deemed unconstitutional by the US Supreme Court and have since been rescinded. In the ensuing decades, policies accommodating dual citizenship were the norm. More recently, however, the very legitimacy of the concept of national citizenship has been called into question.

The ideology of universalism, which seeks to eliminate national borders and identities in order to create a homogenous global community, has captured the imagination of many in the West. Within such an intellectual framework, all distinctions and differences between peoples and cultures are downplayed, rendered insignificant, and recast as mere superficial features. As the French political philosopher, Pierre Manent, in his book *Democracy Without Nations: The Fate of Self-Government in*

---

1   Samuel P. Huntington, *Who Are We? The Challenge to America's National Identity* (Simon & Schuster, 2004), p. 204.

Europe, puts it, "It is no longer simply a matter of recognizing and respecting the humanity of each human being. We are required to see *the other as the same as ourselves*."[2]

Accordingly, the idea of dual citizenship is no longer the problem; exclusive citizenship is. In some circles, the idea that a nation has a unique character, culture, and value system that is worth preserving and a source of pride has come to be seen as primitive. In an age, says Manent, where no culture is better than the next, "the only blameworthy human conduct for us is what used to be called 'conversion.' There is no longer any legitimate transformation or change of mind, because no one preference is more legitimate than any other."[3] Moreover, the expectation that an individual, in order to obtain citizenship, should have to affirm a specific set of values and principles, while implicitly rejecting others, is seen as a violation of human dignity. As a result of these intellectual shifts, citizenship in practice, as Huntington explains, is no longer understood as a demonstrable act of conviction and identification, but as a ticket to receiving benefits.[4]

This extreme universalism is anathema to Judaism; healthy nationalism and genuine citizenship undergirds our civilization. This is seen no more clearly in the Torah than in the laws of the *korban Pesach*. In this *parashah*, Hashem instructs Moshe Rabbeinu concerning the *korban Pesach* numerous times. In the third instance, Moshe is told:

> *When a convert sojourns among you, he shall make the Pesach-offering for Hashem; each of his males shall be circumcised, and then he may draw near to perform it and he shall be like the citizen of the land.*[5]

Rashi, aware of the text's implication, precludes the thought that, as part of the conversion process, a convert would have to bring a *korban*

---

2   Pierre Manent, *Democracy Without Nations? The Fate of Self-Government in Europe* (ISI Books, 2013), p. 5.
3   Ibid., p. 8.
4   Samuel P. Huntington, *Who Are We? The Challenge to America's National Identity* (Simon & Schuster, 2004), pp. 212, 219.
5   *Shemos* 12:48.

Pesach — at any point in the calendar year — to ratify his conversion.[6] But if the Torah does not intend for every convert to offer a *korban Pesach* as part of the conversion process, and only means to include a convert in the annual *korban Pesach* ritual, why does the Torah present it in a way that is misleading? My *rebbi*, Rabbi Michael Rosensweig, answers that the Torah presents the *korban Pesach* in the way that it does to convey a conceptual truth: the *korban Pesach* is a conversion ritual, on a collective scale. Just like each prospective convert in the times of the Beis Hamikdash was required to bring a bird-offering as part of the conversion process, Bnei Yisrael in Egypt are called upon to offer the *korban Pesach* as part of their collective conversion and assumption of citizenship in the Jewish polity.

Conversion to Judaism requires not only circumcision (for males) and immersion in a mikvah, but an expressed desire to take refuge under Hashem's protective wings, an acceptance of the commandments, and the rejection of all other ways of life. Because conversion is such a radical undertaking and dramatic break from one's past, every convert is legally considered like a newborn child: they are forgiven for past sins, they theoretically can marry members of their family of origin (if they were to convert), and they theoretically lose the right to inherit their gentile relatives.[7]

Because the *korban Pesach* is a virtual act of conversion, it, too, must reflect the participant's firm commitment to the nation of Israel, unequivocal acceptance of the tenets of Judaism, and implied rejection of other value systems. That the *korban Pesach* demands conviction and cannot even countenance any ambiguity and uncertainty, is reflected in the prerequisites to participate in the *korban Pesach*. In the very same passage quoted above, Moshe is told:

> *This is the decree of the Pesach-offering: no alienated person may eat from it…A toshav and sachir may not eat from it…no uncircumcised male may eat of it.*[8]

---

6   Commentary to ibid.
7   BT *Yevamos* 22a and 48b; BT *Kiddushin* 17b.
8   *Shemos* 12:43–48.

All four of these exclusions, the alienated person, the *toshav*, the *sachir*, and the uncircumcised, make up the Torah's own version of an "Oath of Allegiance," which is the prerequisite for full citizenship and participation in the *korban Pesach*. Even though an "alienated person" — a heretic — is fundamentally allowed to partake in other sacrificial meat, as well as *terumah*, he is, because of his unwillingness to fully identify with Judaism, barred from eating the *korban Pesach*.[9]

Based on the teachings of our sages, many classic commentators interpret "*toshav*" to mean a *ger toshav* (a resident alien), and "*sachir*" to mean a convert who has undergone circumcision but has yet to immerse himself. Both of these individuals can be viewed as quasi-converts. According to many sages and commentators, the *ger toshav* is not a righteous gentile, but a type of a Jewish convert, one who firmly believes in Hashem and in the teachings of the Torah, and who wants to fully convert and assume a comprehensive Jewish lifestyle. The only thing holding him back, though, is that he cannot give up nonkosher food.[10] Consequently, he is not permitted to fully convert and marry a Jewish woman. In the meantime, however, until he weans himself off his nonkosher diet, he formally assumes the status of *ger toshav*, is encouraged to live in the Land of Israel,[11] and is enjoined to observe the Shabbos and as many other mitzvos as he can.[12] The *sachir*, who has been circumcised for the sake of conversion, but has not yet healed to be allowed to immerse in the mikvah, is similarly considered quasi-Jewish, and, he too, it is axiomatically assumed, must keep the Shabbos and abide by all the mitzvos.[13]

Still, if the *toshav* and *sachir* are quasi-converts (or quasi-Jews) why

---

9   BT *Pesachim* 96a.
10 BT *Avodah Zarah* 64b, based on *Devarim* 14:21. See also *Tosafos*, BT *Avodah Zarah* 20a, s.v. Lehakdim.
11 *Vayikra* 25:35; *Torah Temimah* to *Devarim* 23:17.
12 BT *Yevamos* 48b, *Kerisos* 9a; BT *Avodah Zarah* ibid. See also *Biur Halachah* 303:3.
13 For example, see Responsa *Binyan Tzion* 91.

can't they partake in the *korban Pesach*? It seems that the answer is that when it comes to conversion and citizenship, anything less than an unequivocal affirmation of identification and loyalty to the cause is unacceptable. Even though the only reason the *ger toshav* has not yet completed the conversion process is because he can't resist eating non-kosher, and not due to any ideological reasons, the impression of doubt and possible lack of conviction disqualifies him from full citizenship and participation in the *korban Pesach*. Likewise, although the *sachir* is prevented from consummating his conversion due to therapeutic reasons, the delay creates ambiguity and invites uncertainty about his level of commitment and rejection of his past.

For the same reason, the uncircumcised person listed in the *pasuk* is ineligible for the *korban Pesach*. According to *Rashi*, the *pasuk* does not refer to an individual who flagrantly disregards the law; rather, it refers to an individual whose brother died due to circumcision.[14] As a necessary precaution, he was never circumcised. Despite his reasonable excuse and good intentions, the objective fact that he is uncircumcised undermines his citizenship in that he failed to demonstrate his allegiance unequivocally.

According to the *Rambam*, in Egypt, the *korban Pesach* was a mechanism to test Bnei Yisrael's loyalties and to determine how they self-identified: as Egyptians or as Jews?[15] Once we entered the land, the *korban Pesach* was an annual reaffirmation of our past collective conversion and inherited citizenship. Today, in the absence of its practice, the laws and memory of the *korban Pesach* fortify us against those who seek to delegitimize our national aspirations. Moreover, the *korban Pesach* sheds light on the true nature of the movement for human unification.

The underlying motive behind the spirit of universalism is twofold, and it corresponds to every animal's basic drives: pleasure and self-preservation. As in the days of old, when idolaters practiced paganism to justify their licentiousness and to propitiate the gods for protection

---

14   Commentary to *Shemos* 12:48.
15   *Guide for the Perplexed* 3:46.

and prosperity, universalists today have been pushing their agenda to secure the same things:

- The claim of sameness despite obvious differences implies that there is no objective standard by which to assess and adjudicate between the different cultures, values, and lifestyles. Downplaying differences that were once viewed as fundamental, reflects and fosters the notion that there are no absolute truths and that every moral claim is relative. The gains of cultural and moral relativism are, of course, obvious: anything goes. To paraphrase Dostoyevsky, "Without nationalism and culturalism, everything is permissible."
- While the removal of moral restrictions and restraints is not readily acknowledged by the universalists, the goal of self-preservation is. The stated goal of universalism and its dream of a global community is perpetual peace. People only go to war with the perceived 'other' and over perceived significant differences. If one socially engineers sameness, then the pretext for war and its horrors ceases to exist.

Ironically, but not surprisingly, it is the universalists who are the primitive ones. Just as the ancient Egyptians debased themselves by worshipping false and futile gods for the primitive gains of self-gratification and self-preservation, contemporary universalists (by trying to socially engineer humans toward homogeneity in the quest to avoid war) demean their members. This is so, because, as the Torah (which always talks in terms of nationalities) makes clear, national identity is part of what makes us fully human. Hashem's abiding interest in the preservation of the diverse nations of the world manifests itself in many ways, for example:

- On the Festival of *Sukkos*, we are enjoined to sacrifice seventy bulls on behalf of the "Seventy Gentile Nations," to atone for their sins.[16]

---

16 BT *Sukkos* 55b. For a more nuanced approach, see *Rashi's* commentary to *Bamidbar* 29:13.

- When thirty of the first original "Seventy Gentile Nations" were wiped out as a consequence for having participated in the building of the Tower of Bavel, Hashem deliberately establishes thirty new nations in their place.[17]
- At Har Sinai, the *Aseres HaDibros* were spoken by Hashem in all seventy original languages.[18]
- Adam HaRishon is inspired to give each animal a name in all seventy original languages.[19] [20]

The sociologist Peter L. Berger, in *The Social Construction of Reality*, posits that what makes man uniquely different than animals is his ability to construct his own environment, which is not natural but social and cultural. As Berger says, "Solitary human being is being on the animal level…Man's specific humanity and his sociality are inextricably intertwined. *Homo sapien* is always, and in the same measure, *homo socius*."[21] Based on the Torah's emphasis on nations and their indispensable role in this world, we can say that, *homo sapien* is always, and in the same measure, *homo natio*.

In the final analysis, a utopian society that achieves its lofty goals at the expense of its members' humanity is dystopian. As it did in ancient Egypt, the *korban Pesach* beckons us to preserve our human dignity (and nationality) against the pernicious ideologies of the day that attempt to undermine it.

---

17 *Bereishis Rabbah* 38:10. See also *Devarim* 32:8.
18 BT *Shabbos* 88b. See also *Tosafos*, BT *Berachos* 13a, s.v. *B'lashon*.
19 Cited in Menachem M. Kasher, *Torah Shelemah: Volume I* (Torah Shelemah Institute, 1992), p. 239.
20 Even in Messianic Times and in the End of Days distinct nationalities will be preserved. For two examples, see *Sefer Zechariah* 14:16–19 and BT *Avodah Zarah* 2a–b.
21 Peter L. Berger and Thomas Luckmann, *The Social Construction of Reality* (Anchor Books, 1967), p. 51.

Beshalach

Singing Angels, Robots, and Humans

ALTHOUGH THE *PASUK*, "And one did not draw near the other all night,"[1] describes the tense military situation that existed between Am Yisrael and the Egyptians at the banks of the Yam Suf, Rabbi Yochanan perceives an allusion to a drama in Heaven: "The Egyptians were drowning in the sea. At the same time, the angels wanted to sing before Hashem, and Hashem said to them: 'My creations are drowning and you are singing before me?'"[2] The angels, eager to convene in order to praise Hashem for His triumph over the Egyptians, are chastised by Him and prevented from drawing near to one another to perform. The question, of course, is obvious: If it is inappropriate for the angels to

---

1   *Shemos* 14:10.
2   BT *Megillah* 10b.

sing songs of praise at the expense of the dying Egyptians, why is Am Yisrael permitted to do so?

Interestingly, there is a different, more expansive version of this episode recorded in the midrash:

> Said Reish Lakish: In three instances the angels requested to sing before Hashem, and He did not let them. They are: at the time of the deluge, by the splitting of the sea, and during the destruction of the Beis Hamikdash.[3]

According to this version of events, which describes the angels' desire to sing not only when Hashem saves Am Yisrael at the sea, but even at times of pure destruction, it is evident that the angels aren't clamoring to sing a spontaneous song to Hashem praising His salvation and triumph. Rather, the angels, despite current events, are poised to sing their daily, scheduled hymns to Hashem.

The criticism directed at the angels, then, isn't because they want to praise Hashem for saving the Jews at the expense of the Egyptians. After all, the Jews themselves erupt in a glorious song of praise and thanksgiving for their salvation, notwithstanding the suffering of the Egyptians (which is consistent with the *pasuk* in *Mishlei* that teaches, "when the wicked perish, there are shouts of joy"[4]). Rather, the angels are rebuked for their inability to balance their daily obligation to praise Hashem with the unexpected and complex turn of events. Despite the ongoing Flood, despite the drowning of the Egyptians, despite the destruction of the Beis Hamikdash, for the angels, it was business as usual. Unlike Bnei Yisrael at the sea, who are able to incorporate and integrate all the divergent aspects and conflicting emotions aroused by the event into a balanced, moving song, specifically composed for that momentous occasion, the angels are ready to offer only their daily, generic hymn to Hashem, apparently oblivious to the human carnage

---

3 *Eichah Rabbah Pesichta* 24.
4 *Sefer Mishlei* 11:10.

at hand. According to Rav Shimon Schwab, this inability of angels to be discerning and discriminating is captured in the well known principle that "no angel is ever assigned more than one mission."[5] Because angels are one-dimensional, they are never given more than one task.[6] Likewise, they are unable to experience events from different perspectives and interpret them holistically.

This fundamental difference between us and angels is like the difference between us and robots. A robot is animated by rules, equations, precise analysis, cold logic, technical procedures. Consequently, it is quite efficient. But, ultimately, robots are limited by their programming. A robot, therefore, would have difficulty making moral or ethical decisions. For how would it go about doing so? Can preprogrammed algorithms discern on a case-by-case basis and weigh all aspects of an event to reach a resolution? What kind of valuations would be assigned to the numerous ethical principles that present themselves in any given situation? And how would the programmer anticipate the countless and varied scenarios that would be encountered? Because of this limitation, robots — and angels — cannot mediate clashing values or conflicting human emotions, they cannot appreciate ambiguity and nuance, and they cannot grasp the singularity of certain situations.

For this reason, not only are the angels misguided in wanting to carry out their daily rendition despite the rising human death toll, they are also confused about Hashem's justice. According to the *Zohar*, as the sea engulfs the Egyptians, the prosecuting angels petition, "These [the Jewish People] are idol-worshipers, and these [the Egyptians] are idol-worshipers! Why save one and drown the other?!"

The comment is shocking. The angels can't discern the fundamental difference between the pagan Egyptians, on the one hand, and the children of Avraham, Yitzchak, and Yaakov, on the other? True, the Jews are presently idolators, but this is due to compelling circumstances: their prolonged enslavement and powerlessness.

---

5   BT *Bava Metzia* 86b.
6   Shimon Schwab, *Maayan Beth ha-Sho'eva* (Mesorah, 2000), p. 164.

It's no wonder, too, as our sages tell us elsewhere,[7] that the angels once wondered out loud why, unlike on every other Yom Tov, we don't recite *Hallel* on Rosh Hashanah and Yom Kippur. They had to be instructed by Hashem that when the Books of Life and Death are opened before the King, *Hallel* is inappropriate. The angels, it seems, just don't get it. Because they can't.

Bnei Yisrael, however, do. As does Yisro. When Moshe Rabbeinu tells his father-in-law all that Hashem had done to Pharaoh and the Egyptians, the Torah records Yisro's reaction: "*Vayichad* Yisro over all the goodness that Hashem had done for Israel, that He rescued him from the hand of Egypt."[8] After *Rashi* translates "*Vayichad*" according to its plain-sense meaning, "and Yisro rejoiced," he offers another interpretation in the opposite direction: "Yisro's flesh became prickly — he developed *chidudim*, goosebumps — because he was aggrieved over the destruction of the Egyptians."[9] The contradictory interpretations can be reconciled by considering the complexity of the event. Because Bnei Yisrael's salvation came at the expense of countless lives, and to people with whom Yisro identified, his joy was tempered. He had mixed feelings. So when the Torah expresses Yisro's joy, the Torah deviates from the standard word for rejoicing, "*va'yismach*," in order to capture his complicated, nuanced response.

Often, we have a tendency to think like angels. We are more comfortable with ideas and realities that are clear-cut and simple, and we therefore don't approach issues and circumstances the way they really are: complex and complicated. We steer clear of ambiguity and nuance, we avoid thinking in shades and degrees, and we disdain living with uncertainty and perpetual tensions. Instead, we embrace black-and-white, all-or-nothing, one-dimensional thinking. In order to avoid confronting new realities with their host of concomitant challenges and indeterminate opportunities, we will even repeat narratives that were

---

7   BT *Arachin* 10b.
8   *Shemos* 18:9.
9   Commentary to ibid.

first formulated years ago, when circumstances were vastly different. Like angels, we ignore contemporary circumstances and act and speak as if nothing has changed. We do so, all to avoid breaking our sense of security and bubble of complacency.

The Torah, as we know, was not given to angels. It was gifted to us. In order to fulfill our destiny, we will have to learn how to face facts and confront reality, with all its anxieties, ambiguities, and uncertainties. And with all its promise. *Az Yashir*, then, and only then, we will all sing, one more time.

Yisro

The Difference Between Yisro and Balak

BOTH ARE NON-JEWISH.

Each one has a *parashah* named after him.

Yet, the comparisons end there. Yisro attaches himself to Am Yisrael; Balak attacks.

Let us explore why Yisro and Balak have such drastically different reactions to the same events. Why is one inspired while the other is threatened by Am Yisrael's emergence on the international stage?

The *Rambam* observes that *Targum Onkelos* invariably deviates from the literal translation of any word or phrase that describes Hashem in anthropomorphic terms. In order to preclude any misunderstanding and to ensure that the uninitiated do not attribute corporeality to Hashem, *Onkelos*, says the *Rambam*, always renders the *pasuk* in a nonliteral way. For example, in this *parashah*, when the Torah describes Hashem's descent upon Har Sinai as, "*Vayered Hashem al Har Sinai*,"[1] *Onkelos* doesn't render *"vayered"* as, "And Hashem descended." Rather, he translates it as, "And Hashem manifested on Har Sinai."[2] This way, no one will mistakenly think that Hashem has a physical body and functions like a human.[3]

The *Maharal* extends this idea to include any translation that would demean Hashem's honor. For example, whenever the Torah records that Hashem heard something, *Onkelos* avoids offering a literal translation. Hearing is an act of dependency: there is a dialogue between two parties, with the implication that the listener is lacking and needs something 'inserted' into his ear. However, Hashem doesn't need another's perspective, position, instruction, or advice. To suggest otherwise, is disrespectful.[4] So when the Torah records that Hashem hears something, *Onkelos* invariably inserts the word "before" in his translation: "And the voice of the lad was heard *before* G-d."[5] Or, "If the orphan will cry out to Me, I shall *receive before* Me his cry."[6] By doing so, *Onkelos* distances Hashem from the natural act of hearing and portrays the event more like a king receiving an audience in his throne room.

However, observes the *Maharal*, *Onkelos* is not as vigilant when it comes to the act of seeing.[7] Sometimes, when the Torah describes Hashem seeing, *Onkelos* does slightly alter the meaning, but, in other places, he feels comfortable translating the word literally, as in, "Hashem saw (*chazah*) that the wickedness was great upon the earth."[8] Why? What's the difference between hearing and seeing? Unlike hearing, seeing is an act of independence. It is done alone. The individual sees things exclusively from his vantage point. The act of seeing, therefore,

---

1   *Shemos* 19:20.
2   *Targum* to ibid.
3   *Rambam, Guide for the Perplexed* 1:27.
4   *Tiferes Yisrael* 33, p. 496.
5   *Targum* to *Bereishis* 21:17.
6   *Targum* to *Shemos* 22:22.
7   *Tiferes Yisrael*, ibid.
8   *Targum* to *Bereishis* 6:5.

is compatible with our conception of Hashem, Who is independent and self-sufficient.

At this point, we can better understand why Balak's reaction to Am Yisrael's campaign is radically different than Yisro's. The gulf between them is based on the fundamental distinction between seeing (*re'iyah*) and hearing (*shemiyah*).

Balak apprehends Am Yisrael through the act of seeing: "Balak the son of Zippor *saw* (*vayar*) all that Israel had done to the Emorim."[9] Because Balak relates to Am Yisrael through the act of seeing, he experiences their emergence and success only from his own perspective, independently. Because Balak sees Am Yisrael only in his own terms, he sees them narrowly and, therefore, as a threat. So he attacks.

But not Yisro.

"Yisro, the priest of Midian, Moshe's father-in-law, *heard* (*Vayishma*) of all that G-d had done for Moshe, and for Israel His people, and that Hashem had brought Israel out of Egypt."[10] Unlike Balak, Yisro apprehends Am Yisrael through the act of hearing. Yisro, realizing that something unprecedented is unfolding, decides to hear about all the events and all that transpired to Am Yisrael. By doing so, he experiences Am Yisrael from another vantage point, from another perspective. Because Yisro is able to view Am Yisrael's emergence and success more broadly, he is able to perceive them as a metaphor. Not unlike America's early settlers, founding fathers, and the leaders of the Civil Rights Movement, Yisro regards Am Yisrael's journey as a metaphor of hope and redemption for all peoples. Moreover, because he doesn't just behold and interpret these new events in his own terms and ideological framework, Yisro is capable of perceiving that this nation indeed has a new message to offer the world: a system of truth, justice, compassion, and righteousness.

It is no coincidence that we accepted the Torah with the statement, "We will do and *we will listen* (*v'nishma*) to all that Hashem has

---

9 *Bamidbar* 22:2.
10 *Shemos* 18:1.

declared."[11] A life of Torah is lived through the act of hearing. It is predicated on one's willingness to assume the Torah's perspective on all matters. As our sages assert, "The words of Torah do not remain except with someone who has made himself like he doesn't exist."[12] When it comes to success in Torah learning and living, readiness "to do" must be accompanied by a readiness "to listen."

---

11   *Shemos* 24:7.
12   BT *Sotah* 21a.

A Timeless Protest

IT'S STRANGE. WHY is the *parashah* named after Yisro? He appears only briefly in the *parashah*, at the very beginning when he offers sagacious advice to Moshe, and is not to be heard of again until *Sefer Bamidbar*.

Compare this to Noach, Korach, Balak, and Pinchas, which are all fitting names, respectively, for their *parshiyos*:

- Noach is not only present throughout, but is the protagonist of his *parashah*.
- Although Korach only appears in the first third of his *parashah*, the rest of the *parashah*, which affirms the distinction of Aharon and his descendents, is a direct response to Korach's rebellion.
- Balak is the mastermind behind Bilaam's attempted curses, which span his entire *parashah*.
- While Pinchas is only addressed in the very beginning of his *parashah*, the issue of succession and inheritance that begins with him is a theme throughout his *parashah*.

What makes the designation of *"Yisro"* for this *parashah* even more puzzling is the presence of *Matan Torah* and the declaration of the *Aseres HaDibros*. Undoubtedly, these events eclipse Yisro's contribution. Not unlike *parashas Vayeira* and *parashas Vayeishev*, the *parashah* should have been named *parashas "Vayishma"* (and he heard) based on its opening word and phrase, *"Vayishma Yisro kohen Midian* — Yisro, the priest of Midian, heard."[1] The word *vayishma*, whose root word means to

---

1 *Shemos* 18:1.

hear and to accept, perfectly captures the central and climactic moment of the *parashah*: Bnei Yisrael's hearing, receiving, and accepting of the Torah. Why, then, is the *parashah* called *Yisro*?

In Egypt, when Pharaoh is unsure of how to handle his "Jewish Question," he consults, says the midrash, his three advisors:

> *There were three in that plan, Bilaam, Iyov, and Yisro. Bilaam, who devised the plan, was killed. Iyov, who silently consented, was afflicted with suffering. Yisro, who fled in protest of the scheme, was rewarded by having his descendants serve in the Sanhedrin, the supreme Jewish court.*[2]

From Egypt, the midrash continues, Yisro escapes to Midian, where he lives as a prominent and well-respected personality. That is, until he defies them by publicly renouncing their idolatrous culture. As a result, he is ostracized. Then, after hearing about Amalek's vicious attack, Yisro joins the Jewish people, displaying unequivocally where his loyalties lie.

The picture of Yisro that emerges is clear: Yisro is an iconoclast, a person willing to go against convention. Time and time again, Yisro demonstrates that he is not afraid to stand up for what he believes is right, even if his beliefs are unfashionable or politically incorrect, and even at the cost of his own security. Yisro's defining characteristic, his legacy, is his determination to protest.

Is this not the essence of Judaism? Our founder, Avraham Avinu, was known in his day as Avraham Ha'Ivri, because while the whole world stood on one side of the river, he defiantly stood on the other bank. According to our sages, ever since Avraham's iconoclastic stance was institutionalized at Har Sinai, our mere presence on the world stage has elicited gentile animosity because our belief system and lifestyle are a constant reminder that their precious worldviews may be flawed

---

2   BT *Sotah* 11a.

and false.[3] And despite the persecutions we have suffered as a result, we remain determined to carry on our protest in the name of truth, justice, and righteousness.

When we observe the Shabbos, testifying that Hashem created the world in six days and rested on the seventh, we protest against the fashionable belief in a godless world. When we humble ourselves during davening, we protest the hubris of atheism and arrogance of modern liberalism. When we celebrate Pesach and Purim, which commemorate both overt and covert miracles, we protest the pervasive sentiment that the events of our lives are either exclusively controlled by mankind or always explainable by science. When we commit to build families, to give tzedakah, visit the sick, and comfort mourners, all of which exhibit the virtues of selflessness, sacrifice, and compassion, we protest the excess, the greed, and the selfishness that pervade our secular society.

Rabbi Lord Jonathan Sacks observes that: "In Judaism, faith is not acceptance but protest, against the world that is, in the name of the world that is not yet but ought to be."[4] The name *Vayishma* for our *parashah*, therefore, would have missed the mark entirely. *Vayishma* is too passive, implying mere acceptance. Living a life of Torah calls into question and undermines widespread and firmly held ideas, attitudes, and lifestyles. Judaism, from Avraham Avinu to Har Sinai to today, is active protest. It is standing up, at all costs, for what is right. Judaism is Yisro.

---

3   BT *Shabbos* 89a. According to our sages, the Hebrew word *Sinai* (*samech/yud/nun/yud*) is linguistically related to the Hebrew word for hatred, *Sinah* (*sin/nun/aleph/hei*). For purposes of exegesis, the letters *samech* and *sin* are interchangeable.

4   Jonathan Sacks, *To Heal a Fractured World: The Ethics of Responsibility* (Schocken Books, 2005), p. 27.

Mishpatim

When Law Is Not Free from Passion

A RECENT *New York Times* article featured the book *Families and Faith: How Religion Is Passed Down Across Generations*, written by Professor Vern Bengtson. The book is the result of a longitudinal study of 350 families that spans four generations, trying to answer the question: Why do some young people adopt their families' views, while others venture out and adopt their own? The results of his study help shed light on a curious association between the *Kohanim* and our court system.

The beginning of *parashas Mishpatim*, which deals with various tort and civil laws, immediately follows a discussion about the *Mizbei'ach* at the end of *parashas Yisro*. Our sages wonder why the two are juxtaposed and opine that this textual presentation comes to teach that the Great Sanhedrin should be situated on the Temple Mount, adjacent to the

Mizbei'ach.¹ Although at first glance it seems that the Torah's agenda is to place the *Sanhedrin* in the proximity of the inanimate *Mizbei'ach*, it can be demonstrated that the Torah's true objective is to wed the Sanhedrin to the *Kohanim*.

When the *Sefer Mitzvas HaGadol (Sma"g)* discusses the requirement to station the Sanhedrin on the Temple Mount, he only cites the above-mentioned juxtaposition as an afterthought. His primary source is the following *pasuk* in *parashas Shoftim* as support: "If a matter of judgment is difficult for you...You shall come to the *Kohanim* from *Shevet Levi*, and to the judge who will be in those days."² The *Sma"g*'s proof text differs from the exegesis of our sages in two ways:

- While the former emphasizes the position of the Sanhedrin relative to the *Mizbei'ach*, the latter highlights the nexus between the Sanhedrin and the *Kohanim*.
- The *Sma"g*'s source goes further than just demanding that the seat of legislation overlook the sacred activity of the *Kohanim*. The *pasuk* in *Shoftim*, as our sages derive, intimates that the Sanhedrin should ideally include a number of *Kohanim*.

The question is, why? What do the *Kohanim* uniquely contribute to the Sanhedrin's authority that warrants not only their presence, but even their participation? And whatever their special qualities, why is the *Kohanim*'s membership in *Shevet Levi* accentuated in this context?

Let us go back to the study above: Why do some young people adopt their families' views and religious beliefs, while others abandon them. Professor Bengtson's major conclusion is that family bonds matter: "Displays of parental piety, like teaching the right beliefs and practices and keeping strictly to the law can be for naught if the children don't feel close to the parents. Without emotional bonding, these other

---

1   Cited by *Rashi* in his commentary to *Shemos* 21:1.
2   *Devarim* 17:8–9.

factors are not sufficient for transmission."³ Bengtson also found that grandparents have a strong influence on their grandchildren's religious commitment. Moreover, says Bengtson, parents and grandparents who have successfully transmitted their faith to their children and grandchildren weren't "just trying to pass on to their children a checklist of beliefs; there is a kind of passion these parents had for wanting their children to achieve the peace and joy and the hope and the inspiration they had found for themselves."⁴ According to Bengtson, the combination of parental affection and a passion for wanting their loved ones to enjoy what they have experienced (almost) guarantees the transmission of values and lifestyle from one generation to the next.

Perhaps, this is the reason the *Kohanim*'s role goes beyond ritual to encompass legislation and adjudication: because they are best suited to impart Torah values and attitudes. As descendants of Aharon HaKohen, whose love for his fellow man was renowned, *Kohanim* are predisposed to warmth and interpersonal bonding. And as members of *Shevet Levi*, whose passion for what is right and good prevented themselves from partaking in both the sin of the Golden Calf and of the Spies, *Kohanim* are inclined to be impassioned about wanting the best for the people. It's one thing to legislate and enforce practices. It's quite another to deeply believe in the benefit of those practices and to convey to one's constituency a genuine concern for their well-being. For the Great Sanhedrin to be fully effective in its function as the leader and shaper of society it needs a *Kohen*'s touch. This is achieved by its abiding proximity to and inclusion of the *Kohanim*.

The *navi* Yeshayahu declares, "From Tzion will the Torah come forth, and the word of Hashem from Yerushalayim."⁵ The early commentators explain that Tzion is so influential because it is there where the people encounter the *Kohanim*. Yet Am Yisrael, as a whole, is called "a

---

3   Mark Oppenheimer, "Book Explores Ways Faith Is Kept, or Lost, Over Generations," *New York Times*, Jan. 2014.
4   Ibid.
5   *Sefer Yeshayahu* 2:3.

kingdom of *Kohanim*."⁶ And Hillel once taught that we should all be "of the students of Aharon."⁷ This means that we have an obligation to not only pass on to the next generation a checklist of dos and don'ts, but to project an authentic belief in its underlying value system and our passion for our children, grandchildren, nieces, and nephews to achieve the peace and the joy and the hope and the inspiration that we have found for ourselves.

---

6   *Shemos* 19:6.
7   *Pirkei Avos* 1:12.

Terumah

Authenticity vs. Sincerity

SHORTLY AFTER THE destruction of the Second Beis Hamikdash, Rabban Gamliel succeeds Rabbi Yochanan ben Zakai as the leader of the Jewish people. At the time, the city of Yavneh is the Torah center of the nation and the *beis midrash* there comes under Rabban Gamliel's authority. There is much drama in Rabban Gamliel's *beis midrash*, as he and Rabbi Yehoshua become embroiled in an ongoing conflict. As a result of the escalating abuse suffered by Rabbi Yehoshua, Rabban Gamliel is temporarily removed as head of the *beis midrash*. In his stead, the sages appoint Rabbi Elazar ben Azariyah. The new head of the *beis midrash* wastes no time in asserting his newfound authority. On the very day he is appointed, as the Gemara relates, Rabbi Elazar ben Azariyah institutes a new policy:

> On that day they removed the doorkeeper of the beis midrash, and all students were granted permission to enter. For Rabban

> Gamliel, when he was the patriarch, used to stipulate: Any student whose interior is not like his exterior may not enter the beis midrash. That day many benches were added to the beis midrash. Rabbi Yochanan said: Yosef ben Dostai and the rabbis disagree about the matter. One says four hundred benches were added, and the other says seven hundred benches.[1]

From the continuation of the Gemara, it is evident that this new policy is well received, if not embraced by the sages. But why? Rabban Gamliel's concern that an open-door policy would attract disingenuous students to the *beis midrash* is a valid one. The standard of *"tocho k'baro"* — authenticity, acting consistently in public and in private, outwardly and inwardly, is not a personal preference of Rabban Gamliel; the Torah itself establishes this standard in this *parashah*.

After Moshe Rabbeinu is instructed to fashion the *Aron* out of wood, he is instructed to plate the wood's surface, on the outside and inside, with gold. Commenting on this design, our sages state that any scholar whose interior is not like his exterior (*sh'ein tocho k'baro*) — whose inside does not have the same luster as his outside — is not a scholar. Some even go further and describe such an individual as "a disgusting one."[2] But if this is the case, why is Rabbi Elazar ben Azariyah permissive? Why does he seemingly lower the standards? Doesn't he value authenticity?

This question of what the correct attitude toward proper comportment should be persists till this day. We live in an age that has been described as an "Age of Authenticity." Everyone, it seems, aspires to live by the motto, "Be true to yourself." Conformity is sinful, and the greatest evil is to pretend you are something that you are not. Still, as Adam Grant once observed in the *New York Times*, we don't really want to be authentic all the time. After all, there are parts of our personality that we don't want to advertise. We all, now and then, hide what we

---

1   BT *Berachos* 28a.
2   BT *Yoma* 72b.

actually think or feel to avoid being shamed or shunned. To truly live by the motto "Be yourself," would be foolish, if not socially fatal. But in the "Age of Authenticity" when we all want to be genuine, acting disingenuously seems wrong. So what is one to do when both authenticity and duplicity are not lifestyles of choice? Grant finds an answer to this dilemma in the works of the literary critic Lionel Trilling: sincerity. Grant explains how living with sincerity is different than living with authenticity as follows:

> *Instead of searching for our inner selves and then making a concerted effort to express them, Trilling urged us to start with our outer selves. Pay attention to how we present ourselves to others, and then strive to be the people we claim to be. Rather than changing from the inside out, you bring the outside in.*[3]

This acceptable strategy of sincerity, of genuinely wanting to live up to the way one acts and presents himself, was articulated by the *Sefer HaChinuch* when he formulated his oft-quoted phrase, "A man's heart and thoughts are always drawn after his deeds."[4] The *Chinuch* didn't think it was disingenuous or wrong to behave out of character in order to grow accustomed to a Torah lifestyle and to develop, over time, Torah sensibilities and attitudes. His acceptance of sincerity over authenticity reflects a realistic view that religious excellence is not achieved instantaneously. Instead, it is a lifelong process, marked by gradual change. Only after a lifetime of study and self-examination and habituation can we be expected to approach the person we are meant to become.

Perhaps this dichotomy between authenticity and sincerity explains the different policies of Rabban Gamliel and Rabbi Elazar ben Azariyah, respectively. Both great sages agree that a person who is not *tocho k'baro*, whose interior is incompatible with his exterior, does not belong in

---

3   Adam Grant, "Unless You're Oprah, 'Be Yourself' is Terrible Advice," *New York Times*, June 2016.
4   *Sefer HaChinuch* 16.

the *beis midrash*. They disagree, however, regarding how to define the category of *tocho k'baro*:

- Rabban Gamliel's yardstick is authenticity. For him, any outward observance that does not accurately reflect one's inner nature is deemed inconsistent and incongruous, and therefore, disingenuous. Consequently, there is no room for leniency.
- Rabbi Elazar ben Azariyah, on the other hand, measures *tocho k'baro* with the standard of sincerity. To be sure, deceitful behavior is disingenuous. And a person who conducts himself in such a manner is not *tocho k'baro*, is ineligible to enter the *beis midrash*, and may even be considered loathsome. Still, outward behavior that does not reflect one's inner nature because the process of change has not yet been completed is not viewed as inconsistent and incongruous. Rather, the intended goal of excellence, represented by the outward behavior, creates an internal coherence and compatibility. Anyone whose behavior fits this description is indeed considered *tocho k'baro*.

Rabban Gamliel's strict policy, then, has unintended consequences: By keeping out anyone whose interior is not like his exterior, Rabban Gamliel excludes individuals who are not disingenuous and inauthentic, but merely incomplete.

Rabbi Elazar ben Azariyah's method of sincerity is also intimated in the structure of the *Aron* itself. The midrash is bothered why, if the two golden elements of the *Aron* represent *tocho k'baro*, is the wooden material in the middle used at all? Ostensibly, the midrash wonders, two pieces of gold, an outer one and an inner one, would suffice to convey the moral message.[5]

According to Rabbi Elazar ben Azariyah, however, such a design champions the standard of authenticity and belies the value of sincerity. Two pieces of gold alone would suggest that only someone whose exterior matches his interior is deemed worthy. Instead, the gold-wood-gold

---

5   *Mishnas Rabbi Eliezer* 13.

design of the *Aron* symbolizes sincerity: The outer gold represents the genuine ambition for excellence. The inner gold represents the inner self that has been already transformed by abiding by higher standards. The wood in the middle represents the unrefined parts of one's personality, the not yet, but hoped-for areas of excellence.

Rabbi Elazar ben Azariyah, of all people, understood that excellence is not expected to be attained instantaneously, nor in one's youth. Although he was a great candidate for the position of *nasi* — he was wise, independently wealthy, and a direct descendant of Ezra HaSofer, there was one problem. As his wife pointed out to him, he was relatively young, and he looked it.

Miraculously, that obstacle was overcome when, by the very next morning, Rabbi Elazar ben Azariyah awoke with a countenance of an elderly sage, having gone gray overnight. It was then that he famously declared, "It is as if I am seventy years old."[6] There was no one in the *beis midrash* whose exterior misrepresented his interior more than Rabbi Elazar ben Azariyah. This did not deter him, for his sagacious beard accurately reflected his genuine desire to one day be an outstanding *talmid chacham*. The sincerity with which Rabbi Elazar ben Azariyah comported himself informed his policy. In his first day of office, he courageously went against precedent to ensure that no student who lived with sincerity be left on the outside looking in.

May we all continue on our lifelong journeys toward religious, spiritual, and moral excellence with the soothing knowledge that we are all always welcome into the *beis midrash* of Rabbi Elazar ben Azariyah.

---

6   BT *Berachos* 28a.

Tetzaveh

The Sights and Sounds of Mitzvos

ALONG THE HEM of the *Kohen Gadol*'s robe was sewn a pattern of pomegranates and bells. "It shall be on Aharon when he performs the service, and its sound shall be heard when he enters the Holy before the Lord and when he leaves, so that he will not die."[1] The *Ksav V'Kabbalah*, Rav Yaakov Tzvi Mecklenburg, explains that the pomegranate-bells serve the same function as tzitzis: a constant reminder of the mitzvos. The countless seeds of a pomegranate symbolize the 613 mitzvos. While tzitzis grab our attention through our sense of sight, the bells capture the *Kohen Gadol*'s attention through his sense of hearing. Due to his greater responsibilities, the *Kohen Gadol* needs an additional reminder of the mitzvos and his mission.[2]

---

1 *Shemos* 28:35.
2 Commentary to ibid.

Why, though, does the Torah employ a different primary sense than the one used by tzitzis? Even if the *Kohen Gadol* indeed requires an individualized reminder of the mitzvos, why doesn't the Torah simply add a visual cue to his raiments? Why switch to an audio aid? On the other hand, if audio is more effective, why are we given the visual aid of tzitzis?

Unlike the majority of other mitzvos, the Torah spells out in clear terms the objective of tzitzis: "This shall be fringes for you, and when you see it, you will remember all the commandments of the Lord to perform them, and you shall not wander after your hearts and after your eyes after which you are going astray."[3] Rav Shimshon Raphael Hirsch, sensitive to the *pasuk*'s stress on the protective factor of tzitzis from self-gratifying behaviors, understands the mitzvah of tzitzis in the broader context of an ongoing battle between the visible and invisible. Unlike the idols of yesteryear and empirical science of today, Hashem is uniquely invisible:

> *Rabban Gamliel was once asked by a pagan, "Where is G-d to be found?" He answered, "I don't know." The pagan continued, "Of what avail are all your daily prayers and your wisdom, if you do not even know where He is?"*
>
> *To which Rabban Gamliel replied, "The Holy and Blessed One sees all His creatures, but they cannot see Him, as it is written, 'No man can see Me and live.'"*[4]

This exchange highlights that, for the average person, it is intellectually and psychologically difficult to worship an invisible deity. As Ernest Becker writes, the whole point of an idol or a Pharaoh to worship, not to mention the appeal of modern science, is that it provides its followers with a sense of control and security. With an invisible G-d, you never know where you stand in His eyes. Moreover, says Becker,

---

3   *Devarim* 15:39.
4   *Midrash Tehillim* 103:5.

while everyone else flaunts their visible gods or scientific proofs, the pure monotheist is left with no visual evidence with which to counter.[5]

And, continues Rav Hirsch, not only is Hashem invisible, but, for all intents and purposes, the one-time revelation of our laws at Har Sinai is invisible, too. As an event of the past, lacking any physical trace, we are unable to behold the revelation. To make matters worse, the very primitive desires that Hashem and His Torah intend to restrain and regulate are aroused and encouraged by visible stimuli all around us. Whereas our eyes cannot see Hashem and the source of His law, our eyes are constantly enticed by the sensual pleasures everywhere we turn. Because of this struggle, between the visible and invisible, the Torah, says Rav Hirsch, commands us to place tzitzis on our garments.

> *But G-d does not wish you to follow the course prompted by your heart or your eye, and so He has given you a means whereby in the present, visible world you will always have a visible reminder of G-d — Himself invisible — and a present reminder of His law given in the past.*
>
> *In short, a means that directs your attention from the visible to the invisible and brings the past palpably before you in the present. This means is tzitzis; indeed, it is called tzitzis from the root meaning 'to appear in visible form.'*[6]

According to Rav Hirsch, we fight the visible with the visible, to remember the One Who Is Invisible.

As sharp as Rav Hirsch's interpretation is, to our Jewish sensibilities it is quite jarring. The predominant theme of the Torah is iconoclasm, the outright rejection of idols, images, visual aids, and the like. And the defining characteristic of the Revelation at Har Sinai, we are reminded by Moshe in his valedictory, is that we saw no vision of Hashem: "Hashem spoke to you out of the midst of the fire; you heard the sound

---

5   Ernest Becker, *Escape From Evil* (Free Press, 1975), p. 53.
6   Shimshon Raphael Hirsch, *Horeb: A Philosophy of Jewish Laws and Observances*, p. 181.

of the words, but saw no image, just a voice."[7] We are the "People of the Book" for a good reason; we don't rely on our sense of sight as other religions do, but on our sense of hearing, as we listen to the Word of Hashem, as recorded in His Torah. The mitzvah of tzitzis, then, designed to remind us of and represent Hashem and His mitzvos, is seemingly incongruous with the rest of the Torah.

Perforce, the mitzvah of tzitzis, which serves as a visual religious aid, is a concession to human weakness. Because Hashem wired us to respond to and find security in what we can see and touch, worshipping an invisible being can be quite challenging. Although Hashem has demanded us to overcome our primitive needs, prohibiting us from even fashioning representations of Himself to worship, Hashem compromises wherever He sees fit.

For example, the Torah permits the *eved ivri* to remain with his mortal master, even after his six years of service are up. For some individuals, it is too psychologically demanding to give up the security that comes with having a concrete, visible, and tangible master. At the same time that the Torah concedes to the *eved ivri*'s primitive needs, it reminds him of the Torah's true expectations: to become mature enough and capable of serving an invisible Master Who once made His Voice heard on Har Sinai. This is why, of all parts of the body, the *eved ivri*'s ear is pierced, to reflect his failure to rely on his sense of hearing.

Likewise, in the struggle against our base desires, which are only strengthened by all the visible stimuli surrounding us, Hashem allows us to marshal the visible tzitzis to remind us of the Invisible. But just because the Torah gives in to our current weaknesses, that doesn't mean the Torah gives up on the ideal.

For this reason, the *Kohen Gadol* — the ideal Jew — is reminded of Hashem not with sight but with sound. The *Kohen Gadol* struggles against the visible with the auditory. By way of the pomegranate-bells, the *Kohen Gadol* fights the visible with the invisible, to remember the Invisible. Utilizing sound instead of sight both reflects and fosters the

---

7   *Devarim* 4:12.

Kohen Gadol's ability to perceive and serve what cannot be seen and touched and measured: the One Who Is Invisible.

As Jews, we are the Tzitzis and Pomegranate-Bells of the world. Like the pomegranate-bells all along the hem of the robe and the tzitzis hanging off the four corners of the garment, we are spread out over all four corners of the globe. Amalek's mission is to obliterate the world's Tzitzis and Pomegranate-Bells to ensure that Hashem, Who Is invisible, remains so. Whenever we remember what Amalek did to us, and ready ourselves to destroy them, we remember who we are and what our mission is: To enable the world to perceive and serve the One Who Is Invisible.

Ki Sisa

Counting and Complacency

"WHY ARE WE apathetic? With Israel and the world in so much danger, why are we silent? Why aren't we davening?" These were the questions HaRav Moshe Wolfson *shlita*, *rav* of Beis Medrash Emunas Yisrael and *mashgiach ruchani* of Mesivta Torah Vodaath, passionately asked his audience during one of Israel's crises. I would like to suggest a possible explanation behind this perceived silence and complacency, despite Iran's growing nuclear weapons capacity and vicious calls for our destruction.

In the beginning of this *parashah*, Hashem commands Moshe Rabbeinu to count the Jewish people, but to do so indirectly via a *machatzis hashekel*, lest a plague befall the nation. Although implicit in Hashem's instructions here, our sages observe that the prohibition to count Bnei Yisrael directly is made explicit in *Sefer Hoshea*:

> Said R' Elazar: Anyone who counts the people of Israel transgresses a prohibition, as it states, "Yet the number of Bnei Yisrael will be like the sand of the sea, which cannot be measured nor counted."[1] Read not that Bnei Yisrael will be so numerous that they "cannot be counted," but that they "should not be counted."[2]

It is noteworthy that *Rashi*, in various places in Tanach, brings three additional *pesukim* for the source of the prohibition to count Bnei Yisrael. For example, when King Shaul counts his soldiers indirectly by using sheep, *Rashi* explains[3] that he does so because it is prohibited to count Bnei Yisrael, as it says, "and I will make your offspring like the sand of the sea which is too numerous to count."[4] What is remarkable about all four *pesukim*, including the one quoted in the Gemara above, is that they express the promise and blessing that Bnei Yisrael will be so numerous that they will defy being counted. Regarding the three sources he cites, *Rashi*, taking his cue from the Gemara above, rereads each *pasuk* to mean that Bnei Yisrael "*should not* be counted."

Let us ask two basic questions:

1. What is the reason behind this prohibition? Why can't we be counted?
2. Why is the source of prohibition always found in the context of Hashem's promise and blessing to make us so abundant that we will prove impossible to count? In other words, why does the very promise and blessing of proliferation implicitly prohibit us from being counted?

Born in 1930 in a small agricultural village in Northern Hungary, Anna Orenstein arrived at Auschwitz in the summer of 1944 at the age of fourteen. After surviving the war, she immigrated to the United States, where she became a mother of three and a successful child

---

1   *Hoshea* 2:1.
2   BT *Yoma* 22b.
3   Commentary to *Shmuel I* 15:4.
4   *Bereishis* 32:13.

psychologist. She is currently a professor at Harvard. While building a new life in America, Orenstein spoke freely of her lost family, but only divulged bits and pieces of her camp experiences to her children and friends, and only when asked to. One Pesach, however, her daughter, Sharone, came home from college and wanted to create a new way for everyone to participate in the Seder. She asked each member of the family to share what freedom meant to them personally. That night, Orenstein began what was to become an annual Pesach Seder family tradition of sharing her concentration camp experiences with her family. Thirty years later, her family published a collection of her Pesach night tales called *My Mother's Eyes: Holocaust Memories of a Young Girl*. I would like to share with you some of her recollections from the chapter entitled, "The Tattoo":

> *It was a brisk fall morning. Though the air was chilly, we could tell that it would be a "good day," dry and not too cold. We were told early in the morning — I believe during roll call — that we would be receiving tattoos that day. The announcement filled us with optimism. We thought that this was evidence that the Germans intended to keep us alive. We believed that receiving a tattoo meant that we would be sent out of Auschwitz, perhaps to a labor camp, away from the crematoria.*[5]

Orenstein goes on to describe that they were then brought to a building where there were three separate lines leading up to three different girls in uniform, who applied the tattoos. She then describes how, because she desired a nice and neat-looking tattoo, she checked to see which girl did it the best, and then stood in that girl's line. Orenstein concludes the chapter as follows:

> *We were proud of our tattoos, which gave us some sort of identity. We were not registered anywhere with our names,*

---

5 Anna Orenstein, *My Mother's Eyes: Holocaust Memories of a Young Girl* (Emmis Books, 2004), p. 85.

> *birthplaces, and ages. The numbers on our arms identified us, and we gave them added significance by thinking they would save us from extermination.*
>
> *I'm no longer conscious of my tattoo but feel apologetic when I realize that it evokes unpleasant feelings in my friends. The tattoo reminds them of something they would rather forget. Whenever I see them looking at my arm, and I see their discomfort, I want to tell them that the day we received the tattoos was a good day for us, that we considered them to be "passports" to life.*[6]

What emerges from this remarkable testimony is that being numbered, being counted, can create a (false) sense of security and confidence. Although receiving a serial number on her forearm signified she had passed the first selection, it guaranteed nothing.

We, of all the nations of the world, are particularly prone to seeing ourselves as invincible precisely because we have frequently been promised and blessed by Hashem that we will be as numerous as the stars in the sky and the sands on the beach. Counting ourselves would only exacerbate our predisposition to feel indestructible. To be counted would invite not only plague, but economic downturn, military defeat, and moral decay. Because of the inflated sense of confidence and security that comes with being counted, we would become less vigilant, too complacent.

Hashem's promises, though, were never meant to preclude human initiative and input. Hashem never intended for us to become cavalier about our political, military, social, and economic circumstances, let alone our religious and spiritual standing. The Torah, therefore, prohibits the counting of Bnei Yisrael to preclude us from falling into the trap of overreliance on Hashem's promises: Read not that Bnei Yisrael will be so numerous that they "*cannot* be counted," but that they "*should not* be counted."

---

6   Ibid., pp. 87–8.

Perhaps we are not particularly alarmed by Iran's threats and purported nuclear power because we have grown complacent, overconfident. We count our miraculous military victories: '48, '56, '67, and '73, not to mention the 1981 successful bombing of Iraq's nuclear reactor. We count the current growing number of Jews in both Israel and the Diaspora, as we marvel at our proliferation despite the Holocaust and the centuries of the hardships of exile. And we conclude that we are invincible, that the State of Israel is indestructible, and that Hashem Who has promised to increase and bless us, will never let us down. We maintain our equilibrium because we are confident that Hashem will sweep in and save us.

Our sages teach us:

> *Said R' Levi: It was known and revealed to the One Who said the world shall be that Haman would one day weigh out shekalim to harm Israel, therefore, He had Bnei Yisrael's shekalim precede Haman's.*[7]

According to R' Levi, Hashem, in His Omniscience, knew that one day Haman would contrive to destroy us by paying off Achashveirosh with *shekalim*, so He preempted Haman's *shekalim* with the mitzvah of *machatzis hashekel*, to be collected annually at the onset of the month of Adar. Hashem did so because the mitzvah of *machatzis hashekel* reminds us that we are prohibited from ever being counted; that we are not allowed to rely exclusively on Divine promises, taking no responsibility for ourselves; and that Hashem wishes to act through human agency.

In *Megillas Esther*, Mordechai understands this well. Even as he tacitly expresses his unwavering faith in Hashem's salvation, he demands of Esther to intercede. We learn from Mordechai that Hashem's promises were never meant to undermine our sense of responsibility and initiative; instead, they are to serve as a source of confidence, propelling us to action.

---

7   BT *Megillah* 13b.

Pilgrimage, Jews, and Judaism

AT THE END of this *parashah*, the Torah commands us in the mitzvah of *aliyah l'regel*, the thrice-annual pilgrimage to pay homage to Hashem. "Three times during the year all your males shall appear before the Lord, Hashem, the G-d of Israel."[1] What the Torah never says, though, and what is conspicuously missing is: where? Where do we go to go to pay Hashem homage? It's startling that the Torah would leave out this crucial detail.

Moreover, in the very next *pasuk*, the Torah promises that Hashem will expand our borders and that when all males ascend to pay Him homage, no one will exploit our unprotected lands. Based on the connection between our lands and *aliyah l'regel*, the Gemara, in the name of Rav Ami, infers that anyone who does not possess land is not obligated to ascend for the pilgrimage.[2] *Tosafos* draw the following conclusion: Anyone who lives in *chutz l'aretz* is also exempt from *aliyah l'regel*.[3] What?! Isn't the whole point of a pilgrimage to leave your home and hearth, travel far distances at a cost to body and wallet, pay homage to G-d, and then make the long trek back to your house, more inspired than ever?

These difficulties, taken together, suggest that the mitzvah of *aliyah l'regel* is not a "pilgrimage" in the same sense that other religions have journeys to their respective holy sites. In most religions, the site of the pilgrimage has no contemporary political significance. In many others,

---

1   *Shemos* 34:23.
2   BT *Pesachim* 8b.
3   BT *Pesachim* 3b, s.v. *M'alyah*.

there are not one but numerous holy sites where pilgrimages are made to. In others, the individual is expected to make the pilgrimage only once in his lifetime. In some, the pilgrimage is done in a modest fashion by all in order to demonstrate that there is no difference between rich and poor. And in almost all other religions, those who make the pilgrimage assume a special lifetime status of "pilgrim."

In Judaism, *aliyah l'regel* is made to one place and one place only, Hashem's Sanctuary. And according to many authorities, it only applies to the Beis Hamikdash situated in the political capital of the commonwealth.[4] It is to be undertaken not once in a lifetime but thrice *annually*. Moreover, the *aliyah l'regel* is not fulfilled in a socioeconomic vacuum, but in a manner that reflects the individual's everyday, real-life socioeconomic standing, as it says, "everyone according to what he can give."[5] No one receives any kind of lifetime status of "pilgrim."

These numerous differences reflect that Judaism is not a "religion" in the traditional sense, either. Judaism is not just a faith; Judaism is a national, cultural, and religious enterprise — a civilization. The difference between the two is as follows: To live a religious life, one needs no land or country of one's own. One can have faith in anyplace and anywhere. For a civilization to be realized, it needs a land, defined borders, and power.

Because Torah is the blueprint for the ideal human society, encompassing government, economics, social welfare, criminal and family law, medical ethics, and so on, it needs comprehensive political autonomy to be fully realized. The Torah needs sovereign soil to to take root, grow, and flourish.

Perhaps this is why the Torah withholds the location of the destination of our "pilgrimage" until we have conquered, settled, and established comprehensive security in Eretz Yisrael: To underscore that the Beis Hamikdash is not merely the supreme holy site for individual

---

4 See *Ramban* to *Devarim* 16:11 and *Metzudos Dovid* to *Shmuel I* 1:3. For an alternative approach, see BT *Chagigah* 6a and *Ralbag* to *Shmuel I* 1:3.
5 *Devarim* 16:17.

Jews to commune with G-d, but the epicenter of a Torah civilization, where each citizen renews his sense of purpose within the context of the polity.

For the same reason, the mitzvah of *aliyah l'regel* is incumbent only on land-owning citizens of Eretz Yisrael, whose permanence in the land is more certain; it excludes Jews in the Diaspora; is fulfilled not in any holy location, but in a centralized and politically significant site; is woven into the fabric of the annual agricultural and holiday cycle; is experienced in a way that reflects and preserves current socioeconomic distinctions; and does not confer any special lifetime status on its adherents, since it is a taken-for-granted duty of all (male) citizens of the vibrant Jewish Commonwealth. The mitzvah of *aliyah l'regel* is less about the individual's private relationship with Hashem and more about nurturing his sense of belonging to a dynamic Jewish civilization.

Had the mitzvah of *aliyah l'regel* resembled the pilgrimages of most other religions, we would, in all likelihood, have concluded that we can build permanent homes in foreign countries, worship Hashem through Torah study, shul rituals, and communal customs, and be satisfied. Under such an arrangement, we would also grow content with our sporadic and sparse journeys to Yerushalayim, where we would pay homage to Hashem and renew our commitment, only to immediately return home to live our private religious lives in the shadow of our host country. But, as we have seen, such an understanding is a distortion of Judaism. Instead, the Torah's version of "pilgrimage" drives home the message, as some have said, that while *a Jew* can live anywhere, *Judaism* needs a sovereign state in Eretz Yisrael.[6]

---

[6] Compare with the *Ramban*'s comments to *Bereishis* 26:5 and *Vayikra* 18:25.

Zemiros, Shiros, V'Torah

DESPITE THE TORAH'S explicit warning in this *parashah* to count the Jewish people indirectly, "so that there be no plague among them when you number them,"[1] somehow, David HaMelech counts his soldiers directly. Not surprisingly, the country is ravaged by a plague, with the death toll reaching seventy thousand. The midrash is perplexed as to how David HaMelech could have overlooked this cardinal rule.

The midrash answers that Hashem caused David to forget the *pasuk* as a punishment for disrespecting the Torah by referring to it as a *zemirah*, a song. "Your statutes have been my songs (*zemiros*) in the house of my temporary dwelling," exclaims David.[2] For the same infraction, David was also divinely influenced to forget that the *Aron* must be carried on the shoulders of *Kohanim*, and not, as David shockingly did, transported on a wagon.[3]

The midrash, though, creates more questions than it solves. What do disrespecting the Torah, counting the people directly, and transporting the *Aron* inappropriately have to do with one another? Moreover, Hashem Himself calls the Torah a song, "And now, write for yourselves this song (*shirah*), and teach it to the Children of Israel,"[4] which the Gemara says refers to the Torah.[5] How can David be punished for doing the same?

The Gemara records that, once, during a discourse, Rav Yosef announced that, regarding a particular law under discussion, the halachah

---

1   *Shemos* 30:12.
2   *Sefer Tehillim* 119:54.
3   *Midrash Aggadah Shemos* 30:12.
4   *Devarim* 31:19.
5   BT *Nedarim* 38a.

was in accordance with Rabban Shimon ben Gamliel. Rav Yosef's student, Abaye, who had been under the impression that Rabban Shimon ben Gamliel's ruling was undisputed, inferred from Rav Yosef's apparent need to determine normative halachah that, in fact, there are dissenting opinions. When Abaye asks Rav Yosef to clarify who argues with Rabban Shimon ben Gamliel, Rav Yosef rebuffs the inquiry, indicating that such information isn't important. Abaye, undeterred, responds, "Should our learning be reduced to a *zemirah*?"[6] Shocked that his teacher would minimize the significance of a comprehensive presentation of the material, Abaye rhetorically asks, "Should the Torah you teach us be memorized as a ditty, a sing-song just to pass the time?" Not wanting to study Torah casually, for mere entertainment, but seriously and rigorously in order to develop insight, Abaye demands more from his teacher.

Is it a coincidence that Abaye compares superficial, casual Torah study to a "*zemirah*"? Unlikely. What emerges from Abaye's careful choice of words, then, is that there is a fundamental difference between a *zemirah* and a *shirah*:

- A *zemirah*, while melodious, lacks substance. It is composed and sung purely for enjoyment.
- A *shirah*, on the other hand, is substantive and meaningful. It has significance and relevance beyond its entertainment value.

Hashem never calls the Torah a *zemirah*, only a *shirah*. David HaMelech is punished for referring to the Torah as a *zemirah*. Although unintended, *zemirah* implies that, while pleasant, the Torah is superficial and not practical, and only meant to be studied casually and recreationally. Because David's lapse in judgment could give rise to widespread irreverence for Torah, Hashem causes him to feel the potential impact directly. Caused to forget elementary rules, David demonstrates a cavalier attitude toward both the *Aron* that houses the Torah, and his people who study the Torah. In both cases, the *Aron* and the people are not treated

---

6 BT *Avodah Zarah* 32b.

with the deep respect each deserves: the *Aron* is not mere luggage or cargo, and people are not to be used as a means to satisfy David's ends of self-aggrandizement.

The lesson we learn from this tragic episode is that when it comes to preserving the dignity of the Torah, heightened vigilance is necessary. Because Torah study is so enjoyable, as it was intended to be, the Torah can easily be confused with a *zemirah*, and be studied for pure recreation; even as a diversion. However, the Torah is not a *zemirah* but a *shirah*. It is the blueprint of creation. Each *masechta*, each *sugya*, has broad implications for how to organize our society, as each responds to the essential questions posed by the human condition. As stimulating as Torah study is, what should not be lost in the experience is its unmatched significance and abiding relevance. Let us not forget that the Torah is a singularity. It is not a mere *zemirah* but a sweeping *shirah*.

Vayakhel-Pekudei

Mirror, Mirror, on the Kiyur

LET'S DISCUSS MIRRORS. There are three famous mirrors depicted in children's literature. Can you name them?

1. Magic Mirror — the magical mirror on the wall in the *Snow White* fairy tale.
2. Mirror of Erised — the magical mirror in the *Harry Potter* series.
3. Enchanted Mirror — the magical mirror in the *Beauty and the Beast* fairy tale.

The Magic Mirror, which never tells a lie, is used by the Wicked Queen to inflate her self-image as the most beautiful woman in the world.

The Mirror of Erised, which is Desire spelled backward, shows "nothing more or less than the deepest, most desperate desire of our hearts." Harry, who is orphaned as an infant, sees himself surrounded by his dead parents.

These first two mirrors aren't intriguing. They do what we would expect a magical mirror to do. A regular mirror reflects the viewer's image back to him or her. Looking into a mirror is a self-centered and self-admiring experience. So a magical mirror, we imagine, would enhance this experience. That is exactly what these two magical mirrors do. When the wicked, vain Queen gazes into her infallible mirror, she is reassured that she, indeed, is the fairest of them all. When aching Harry peers into his mirror, it reflects not only his physical self, but his inner self — his hidden desire to be reunited with his mom and dad.

It is the third mirror that should pique our interest. The Beast's Enchanted Mirror doesn't reflect his image back to him; it reveals the image of others.

> *Ashamed of his monstrous form, the Beast concealed himself inside his castle, with a magic mirror as his only window to the outside world.*

When the Beast looks into his mirror, he does not see himself but others. Every time he looks into the mirror, the Beast does not *connect* with himself but with others. This novel quality, however, is not totally unique. The Enchanted Mirror shares this special quality with mirrors found in this *parashah*.

The Torah tells us that Betzalel fashions "the Basin of copper and its stand of copper from the mirrors of the assembled women (*mar'os hatzov'os*) who massed (*tzav'u*) at the door of the Tent of Meeting."[1] Why does the Torah emphasize that the women who bring their mirrors congregate when doing so? Even going so far as to describe and define the mirrors as the "mirrors of the assembled."

According to the *Ibn Ezra*, the Torah is hinting to a mass religious revival movement that began at the time. Numerous women, having overcome their mundane habits, and worldly temptations to attend to their appearance, freely gave away their mirrors, not needing them

---

1   *Shemos* 38:8.

anymore. From here on in, these righteous women's only concern was to come daily to the door of the *Ohel Mo'ed* to daven and to hear religious discourses. Because so many of them underwent this transformation and would convene together at the *Ohel Mo'ed* daily, the Torah refers to their contribution as the "mirrors of the assembled."[2]

The *Ibn Ezra*'s interpretation represents an extreme view on beauty and its relationship with righteousness. For the *Ibn Ezra* there seems to be no middle ground, no balance between an appreciation for feminine beauty, on the one hand, and valuing more substantive and meaningful pursuits, on the other. Either you're in one camp or the other. Adapting the *Ibn Ezra*'s position to our time, we can recast these women's gesture as part of the modern-day "beauty dilemma."

On the one hand, women are pushing for equal recognition alongside men. On the other hand, women are still being portrayed and portraying themselves as objects for men's enjoyment — just look at any advertisement for any product. Ironically, there has been a direct relationship between the rise of feminism and the objectification of women (and men for that matter; both can and are referred to as "eye candy"). Astute feminists have decried this trend, lamenting the fact that as long as women are objectified, genuine equality will never be achieved.

The most ardent feminists have gone to the opposite extreme, rejecting the value of beauty altogether. Feminist pioneer, Susan Brownmiller, back in the eighties, captured this feminist crisis as follows:

> *An unadorned face became the honorable new look of feminism in the early 1970s, and no one was happier with the freedom not to wear makeup than I, yet it could hardly escape my attention that more women supported the Equal Rights Amendment and legal abortion than than those who could walk out of the house without eye shadow. Did I think of them as somewhat pitiable? Yes, I did. Did they bitterly resent the righteous pressure put*

---

2   Commentary to ibid.

> on them to look, in their terms, less attractive? Yes, they did. A more complete breakdown and confusion of aims, goals, and values could not have occurred, and of all the movement rifts I have witnessed, this one remains for me the most poignant and the most difficult to resolve.³

Although the objectification of women is both wrong and harmful, Brownmiller's approach does not resonate, either. Feminine beauty can be valued without objectifying women. They are not mutually exclusive. A woman can pursue higher interests and aims and still appreciate and be admired for her G-d-given beauty. For this reason, perhaps, *Rashi* deviates from the *Ibn Ezra*'s explanation. According to *Rashi*, the opposite occurred: precisely because the women still needed their mirrors their sacrifice was all the more great.⁴

Rashi still has to contend with why the Torah emphasizes that the women assembled by defining the mirrors as the "mirrors of the assembled." Aware of the problem, *Rashi* posits that *"mar'os hatzov'os"* alludes to an earlier episode concerning these mirrors and to a different legion of people. According to the midrash cited by *Rashi*, when the women bring their personal mirrors, Moshe rejects them, finding them offensive. Hashem, however, reassures Moshe and says to him:

> *Accept them, because these are the dearest to Me of all, for by the means of them, the women established legions (tzov'os) of offspring in Egypt. When their husbands would be exhausted by the racking labor, they would go and bring them food and drink, and feed them. Then they would take the mirrors, and each one would view herself with her husband in the mirror, and entice him with words, saying, "I am handsomer than you." By these means they would bring their husbands to desire, and would have relations with them, and conceive and give birth.⁵*

---

3   Susan Brownmiller, *Femininity* (Simon & Schuster, 1984), p. 158.
4   Commentary to *Shemos* 38:8.
5   Ibid.

Vayakhel-Pekudei 151

In Egypt, when the women peer into their mirrors, they don't just see their own reflection; what they see are their husbands' faces. And they see their future children and future generations of Jews. Legions of Jews.

When mirrors are turned only onto the self, gazed upon vainly and in self-absorption, they are distasteful. But when used to see others, when mirrors reflect not the "I" but the "We," they are things of beauty. Ironically, but not surprisingly, by the conclusion of *Beauty and the Beast*, Belle realizes that the Beast, who is kind, gentle, and caring, is genuinely beautiful, while her attractive but arrogant, vain, and selfish suitor is the beast.

Let us conclude our discussions of mirrors with a story about a fifth special mirror:

> *The rav of Leipnik, the Baruch Taam, arranged for his daughter to be married off to the Divrei Chaim of Sanz, then all of fourteen years old. When the Divrei Chaim arrived on the day of the wedding and alighted from the wagon, his future mother-in-law gazed in horror. The Divrei Chaim, unfortunately, was born physically deformed. The Baruch Taam tried in vain to allay his wife's concerns. Told that the shidduch was off, the Divrei Chaim asked if he could speak with the girl privately. Her parents agreed. A few minutes later, the kallah walked out of the room and announced, "Mazel tov!"*
>
> *What happened?*
>
> *The story is told that in the room there was a mirror. The Divrei Chaim asked the girl to stand before the mirror with him. When she looked into the mirror she was startled to see that he appeared tall and handsome. But what shook her was her own reflection: she appeared physically deformed.*
>
> *The Divrei Chaim gently explained that in Shamayim, when their neshamos were destined to be united, he knew that she*

> *was meant to be physically deformed. So he pleaded with Hashem to allow their bodies to switch, to spare her the suffering and humiliation. Needless to say, his prayers were granted and he was born with the physical deformity instead of her.*

When we look in a mirror and what looks back at us is not our own image, but that of another, we behold something magical. When we stare into a mirror not to see what we can gain, but to see what we can give to others, we gaze at something truly beautiful.

Grammar and Greatness

EVERY YEAR, ON March 4th, National Grammar Day is observed in the United States of America. Aside for celebrating the English language, it is a day, writes one reveler, "to write well, speak well, and help others do the same." Many students of grammar use the day to playfully debunk grammar myths. For example, the supposed rule that one may not begin a sentence with the word "And." Although many of us were taught in elementary school to never do this, even a cursory glance of any contemporary book, newspaper, or magazine article shows otherwise.

Speaking of using the word "and" to begin a sentence, the *Rama* records the following prevalent custom:

> Some scribes are careful to arrange for the letter vav (which means "and") to appear at the beginning of each column in a Sefer Torah, and they are called vavei ha'amudim — the hooks of the pillars.[1]

Why we do this, the *Rama* does not tell us. And why, besides for the play on words, we borrow the term "*vavei ha'amudim*," the term found in this *parashah* to describe the tiny hooks used to connect the pillars that comprised the Courtyard of the *Mishkan*, is also left to the imagination.

While we are on the topic of the structure of the Sefer Torah, another question concerning its arrangement comes to mind. *Rashi*, on the very first *pasuk* in the Torah, asks, in the name of R' Yitzchak, why the Torah, a book of mitzvos, begins not with the very first mitzvah given to Bnei

---

1 The Laws of *Sefer Torah, Yoreh Deah* 273:6.

Yisrael as a nation — the mitzvah to sanctify the new moon — but with *Maaseh Bereishis*?[2]

Rashi answers that the Torah begins with *Maaseh Bereishis* to preclude the argument of those who will one day try to undermine the Jewish claim to the Land of Israel. If Hashem created the world and owns it, He can take and give the Land of Israel to whomever He wants.[3] Based on a midrash in this *parashah*, perhaps we can offer a different answer to *Rashi*'s question.

Commenting on the opening *pasuk* in this *parashah*, "These are the accountings of the *Mishkan*,"[4] the midrash records that after the work of the *Mishkan* was completed, Moshe Rabbeinu invites Bnei Yisrael to make an accounting. The audit is conducted and it is discovered that 1,775 shekels are not accounted for. Moshe panics, fearing that his integrity will be questioned. In the end, Hashem enlightens Moshe and draws his attention to the tiny, overlooked hooks — the *vavim ha'amudim*, which were fashioned using those monies. Immediately, we are told, Bnei Yisrael are appeased regarding the construction of the *Mishkan*.[5]

The midrash goes on to address why Moshe felt compelled to conduct an audit in the first place. We are informed that Moshe heard whisperings concerning him. According to one opinion, the people had been deriding him, "Look at his full neck, look at his fatty thighs; he eats and drinks from us! Everything he has is from us!" As soon as Moshe heard this, he demands an audit to prove his integrity. According to another opinion, however, the people had been praising Moshe, "Fortunate is the one who gave birth to him; all his days Hashem speaks with him, all his days he is considered perfect in Hashem's eyes."[6]

If Bnei Yisrael had suspected Moshe of appropriating their donations for his personal needs, it is clear why Moshe calls for an audit. But if

---

2   Commentary to *Bereishis* 1:1.
3   Ibid.
4   *Shemos* 38:21.
5   *Yalkut Shimoni* 415.
6   Ibid.

what Moshe overheard was not scandalous, if the people had merely expressed their admiration of him, why would Moshe conduct an audit?

Because of this difficulty, we can suggest that, according to this latter opinion, it wasn't Moshe who calls for the audit, but Hashem. Having heard the people's excessive praise of Moshe, how they viewed him as perfect and flawless, Hashem fears the people may come to take Moshe's greatness for granted and conclude that Moshe was either born this way or had been invested with it overnight. Such a misunderstanding could have devastating consequences, since it could demoralize and, ultimately, deter them from achieving greatness themselves. Believing that Moshe's greatness had been gifted and not otherwise attainable, they wouldn't aspire to achieve it themselves.

Hashem, therefore, calls for an audit and arranges that the *vavei ha'amudim* be initially overlooked only to be discovered later. Why? In order to impress upon the people that they had overlooked the *vavim* — the "ands" — of Moshe's long and arduous life. Moshe was not born "Moshe Rabbeinu." Nor did he become so instantaneously. Only through *vavei ha'amudim*, through the combination of painful efforts, sacrifices, incremental phases, and timely transformations does Moshe shape himself and achieve greatness. As Martin Luther King Jr. once said, "Change does not roll in on the wheels of inevitability, but comes through continuous struggle."

Once Bnei Yisrael are made aware — through the *vavei ha'amudim* — that Moshe's greatness is something they can strive for, they are appeased regarding the construction of the *Mishkan*, encouraged in knowing that their efforts and sacrifice on behalf of the *Mishkan* will contribute to their long journey to greatness.

In the same vein, the Torah, written with the letter *vav* — the word "and" — at the beginning of each column, begins not with the mitzvah to sanctify the moon, but with *Maaseh Bereishis* to underscore that the Jewish people in Egypt, ready to accept Hashem's mitzvos and fulfill His lofty expectations, did not emerge on the scene instantaneously and in a vacuum. The Am Yisrael we encounter in Egypt is the culmination of a long, arduous process — a series of "ands" — which began at Creation and was continued by the incremental efforts and contributions made by their forefathers.

As we write the scrolls of our lives, may we be sure not to overlook but to include the *vavei ha'amudim* — the "ands" — necessary to achieve intellectual, emotional, and spiritual greatness.

About the Author

RABBI BARUCH DOV BRAUN is the rabbi of Young Israel of Avenue J in Brooklyn, New York. He received his *semichah* from Yeshiva University's Rabbi Isaac Elchanan Theological Seminary (RIETS), where he was a member of the Wexner Kollel Elyon. He is also a *dayan* on the Brooklyn branch of the Manhattan Beth Din for Conversions. After receiving his *semichah*, Rabbi Braun earned a master's degree in social work from New York University's Silver School of Social Work, where he studied social policy and clinical psychology.

Rabbi Braun teaches Gemara and Tanach at DRS HALB High School for Boys and has also lectured throughout the Tristate area. He lives with his wife and children in Brooklyn, New York.

Rabbi Braun welcomes your comments at rabbi.bbraun@gmail.com.